3 347
581
opy 1

MW01205953

SQUASHES:

HOW TO GROW THEM.

A PRACTICAL

TREATISE ON SQUASH CULTURE.

GIVING FULL DETAILS ON EVERY POINT, INCLUDING KEEPING
AND MARKETING THE CROP.

NEW, REVISED, AND ENLARGED EDITION.

BY

JAMES J. H. GREGORY,

INTRODUCER OF THE HUBBARD, MARBLEHEAD, AND BUTMAN SQUASHES.

MARBLEHEAD, MASS.

ILLUSTRATED.

NEW YORK:

ORANGE JUDD COMPANY,

751 BROADWAY.

1883.

SQUASHES:

HOW TO GROW THEM.

A PRACTICAL TREATISE ON SQUASH CULTURE, GIVING FULL DETAILS ON
EVERY POINT, INCLUDING KEEPING AND MARKETING THE CROP.

NEW, REVISED, AND ENLARGED EDITION.

BY

JAMES J. H. GREGORY,

INTRODUCER OF THE HUBBARD, MARBLEHEAD, AND BUTMAN SQUASHES,
MARBLEHEAD, MASS.

ILLUSTRATED.

10365-0

NEW YORK:

ORANGE JUDD COMPANY,

751 BROADWAY.

1883.

INTRODUCTION TO THE NEW AND REVISED EDITION.

Since the first edition of this Treatise was written, the cultivation of the running variety of the squash has spread from New England, to which they were then mostly confined, throughout the Middle and Western States. One result of this is that the markets of the Eastern States are now largely supplied with squashes grown by farmers in the West.

Meanwhile, many new varieties have been introduced, and adopted into general cultivation, that deserved to be illustrated and described ; while many new facts and suggestions on the subject claimed a record ; and it has this seemed best to revise the former treatise, and send out new edition of my Squash Book. The Squash family (*Cucurbitaceæ*) have their habitat in the tropics and warmer portions of the temperate zones; hence they require our hottest seasons to develop them in perfection. With the exception of the Vegetable Marrow, the squash family is almost unknown to our English cousins, as likewise is true of our corn and beans, for though the average temperature of the year is higher with them than with us, yet the extreme hot weather, which these vegetables require, is there wanting.

The introduction of the squash is a matter of the past half century; until within that time, with the exception of the Crookneck, the pumpkins, yellow and black, or " nig ger," were the only varieties cultivated. Though the appetite for squash appears to be in a considerable degree a matter of education, yet it is becoming more and more popular in the vicinity of the large cities of the North, where among vegetables, it now ranks next to the potato.

3

WHAT IS A SQUASH?

In many parts of the South and West, where the fall and winter squashes are not much cultivated, the term "Pumpkin" is used for all the running varieties of the squash or pumpkin family, with the exception of the "Cashaw" class, which includes varieties that are closely allied to the Crookneck. To clearly define what is meant by the word squash in contradistinction from the word pumpkin, as used among market-men, is no very easy matter, as all the varieties, with the exception of the Crooknecks, easily intercross with each other, and in the recently introduced Yokohama, I have reason to believe we have found the connecting link between the Crooknecks and other squashes, thus destroying the reputation which the Crooknecks had hitherto enjoyed of being *the* squashes of the squash family. Grouping all the running varieties together, we express the marketman's idea of a squash, as distinguished from a pumpkin, when we say that all varieties having soft or fleshy stems, either with or without a shell, and all varieties having a hard, woody stem, and without a shell, are squashes; while all having a hard stem and a shell the flesh of which is not bitter, are pumpkins; and all of this latter class, the flesh of which contains a bitter principle, are gourds. In a more general classification, all varieties having a hard shell, are gourds, and those without a shell, are squashes. I had an amusing instance under this system of classification in a lot of seed, ordered from France as "gourds;" on examining them, I found that several of the kinds were varieties of our table squashes. Making a separate classification of the summer varieties, I define such to be squashes, in contradistinction from gourds, as are eatable at any period of their growth. It will be seen that the distinctions I make are more commercial than strictly scientific. What I aim at, is, to so define squashes, pumpkins, and gourds, that experienced market-men, seedmen, and new beginners, may meet on common ground, and clearly understand each other when using these terms.

In passing, I remark, that gourds are far more prolific than either squashes or pumpkins; in some instances more than two score having been grown on a single vine.

SELECTING THE SOIL.

All of the family thrive best, other things equal, in a warm soil, through which the roots can easily find their way. The Hubbard, Butman, and Marblehead squashes appear to attain their highest development in regard to both yield and quality in a soil that is *strong* as well as warm. I would not advise planting in a clay soil under any circumstances, nor on a strong clay loam, unless it be possible by thorough draining and high manuring (for this purpose, long manure is better than fermented), to make such soil light and porous. A drained meadow will often yield enormous squashes, if well manured, but they are apt to be very porous, of poor quality, and poor keepers.

Some years since I planted a piece of rich, black meadow to Hubbards, after manuring liberally in the hills. The result was a tremendous growth of vine, some of the leaves measuring twenty inches in diameter, while the ends of the runners, in their great vigor, lifted themselves by thousands two and three feet above the surface, and with their blunt, arched extremities, looked like a myriad of huge-winged serpents running a race. The squashes were of a lighter green than usual, very large, but, when gathered, proved light in the handling, very porous in structure (cutting like punk), were very poor keepers, and coarse and watery in quality. Though such meadows are thoroughly underdrained, the squashes grown on them are light in proportion to their size, (which always insures poor quality and poor keeping,) unless the meadows have had abundance of sand and loam worked into them, thus adding the proper proportion of silica to the vegetable humus. Some years ago, when the Marrow squash was a novelty, bringing about $4.00 a hundred pounds, one of my townsmen raised some acres on a piece of drained meadow. Only a portion of the meadow had received a good dressing of sand; here the squashes were of about the ordinary size, while on the remainder they grew "as big as barrels." He traded a part of the crop with a peddler for a lot of swine. When the peddler called for the squashes, agreeable to instructions, the father being absent from town, his son showed him the smaller sized lot, say-ing that he had received directions to deliver them, as they were the best of the crop. But the peddler declared that, as he had supplied good pigs, he was entitled to good squashes, and would be put off with no trash. He there-fore loaded his wagons with the "big as a barrel" lot, and left for home. Before many days a friend called, and, with a laugh, asked if he had heard of the result of the squash investment. "There was'nt enough substance in them to hold together until he got home; they were car-ried to market in a few days, and two tons out of five were rotten." If the soil be wet and cold, the growth of the vine is much retarded, and not only is the crop much lessened in size and weight, but at times this singular re-sult is seen—the squash loses its normal form. I have seen a crop of Hubbards grown under such circumstances, all of which were nearly flat at each end, instead of hav-ing the elongations that belong to the normal form.

When two soils of equal natural strength, but one of them being more gravelly in its structure, are heavily and equally manured, I have noticed, in several instances, that the more gravelly piece will give more squashes and less vine than the others.

Unlike some varieties of melons and cucumbers, squashes will do finely on freshly broken sod, which has the ad-vantage (a great one in many localities) of being less infested with bugs, than old tillage soil. The practice of digging holes a foot or two in diameter in patches of turf in waste places, around hedges, or in corners of fields, which, after filling with manure, are planted to squashes, is but a waste of time; the result is, a growth of vine of a few feet in length, the setting of squashes, and then both squash and vine become checked in their growth, as the roots of the vine make vain efforts to penetrate a dense mass of hungry grass roots in search of food, the leaves gradually turn yellow, and before you know it, have entirely disappeared. By pulling on a dead vine, you may drag out a half grown squash hidden in the grass.

If the sod abounds in the pest known as witch, twitch, or quack grass, there is danger that it will overrun the vines. If the grass has not been thoroughly torn up by the cultivator before the vines begin to run, better plow up at once, as the crop will be nearly a failure. Hoeing up and hand pulling will practically amount to nothing under such circumstances. If the sod is not badly run to twitch, there is but little danger, provided the cultivator is faithfully used from the time the vines appear above ground until the runners begin to push. Witch grass can be killed by covering the tops (uncut) with two inches of soil, as I have learned by experiment.

THE MANURE.

The squash vine is a rank feeder. Night soil, barn manure, wood ashes, guano, muscle mud, hen manure, superphosphate of lime, pig manure, sheep manure, fish guano, fish waste—either of these alone, or in compost, is greedily devoured by this miscellaneous feeder. The great error in the cultivating of the squash is to starve it. By many cultivators, when every other crop has had its share, and the manure heap has been used up, a piece of sod is broken for the squash patch, about the only food depended on for the crop being what it can gather from the decay of the fresh turned sod. Under such treatment, the crop is small, the squashes small, and the general result unsatisfactory. Another error of the opposite extreme is one often committed by market gardeners, who have learned that no paying crop can be grown without liberal feeding —who give all the food necessary, but do not allow sufficient room for the extra growth of vines under such culture. Of this latter error I propose to treat under the head of "Planting the Seed."

Night soil, when used, should be mixed with muck and other manures in the form of a compost; though it may be applied fresh, directly to the hill, if sufficient care is taken to mix it thoroughly with the soil. Some years ago, I broke up a piece of land in the spring of the year for squashes, and the location being difficult of access, I used night soil from a vault on the premises, pouring about two bushels into each hill. After we had finished manuring, I sent my hired man, stout Jim Lane, around with his hoe to mix it thoroughly with the soil in the hills. When Jim came back, saying the thing had been thoroughly done, I send him around a second time, to give it another mixing up, and, on his return, sent him around the third time, though the old fellow assured me that it couldn't be improved on, and I had no doubt he had done his work well each time, but, with two bushels of fresh night soil in each, I knew that all the danger lay in one direction. The result was, the vines came up a rich, dark-green, and took right hold of their food.

With the exception of barn manure, it is necessary that each of the manures mentioned above should be well mixed in the soil when used in the hill. When wood ashes are used, they should not be mixed with other manure, until just as it is applied, as this would injure the value of the manure, by setting free the ammonia. When I have used ashes in connection with Peruvian guano, I have been in the habit of putting layer with layer in a wheel-barrow, hurrying it to the hills, and then covering it immediately with soil. Even with all possible hurrying of matters, the strong, pungent smell of the escaping ammonia could be readily detected.

Wood ashes, mixed with fresh night soil in the hill is considerably worse than nothing. Some years ago, aiming to grow some extra large specimens, I selected a favorable location, opened several large hills, and poured into each about a couple of bushels of night soil. Into this I stirred a liberal quantity of wood ashes, acting on the theory that its alkaline properties would serve as a corrective of the rank crudeness of the night soil. I pulled the earth over the hills, and planted my seed. The seed vegetated, but the young plants soon came to a stand still. I applied a little fresh soil to the roots, thinking the manure below might be too strong for the young rootlets to absorb. Still, there was no growth; soon the leaves turned yellow, and the plants died. I opened one hill to find the cause, and there I found cause enough in the presence of a mass having about the size and appearance of an ordinary grindstone; the ashes and night soil in combination had made a hard cement, and the entire contents of each hill could be rolled out in one cake.

HOW MUCH MANURE?

Those who, under the stimulus of a city market, follow market gardening, soon learn one truth that may be set down as an axiom for successful gardening, viz.: that other things equal, it is the last cord of manure that gives the most profit. There is but little danger of giving too much manure to your squash ground, provided the hills are made at a proper distance apart, and the vines are not too numerous.

No prudent man will plant squashes with less than four
1*

cords of barn manure, or its equivalent, to the acre; this is the *minimum*—when squashes are raised as a profitable crop, from six to twenty cords of good manure per acre are used.

Twenty cords to the acre will, I doubt not, sound like a large story to many readers, and it *is* a large quantity, even for the high culture required for successful market gardening, but I have seen that quantity applied, and once, in my own practice, applied thirty-five cords to a little over two acres of squash land, where the soil had been over-cropped, (or rather under-fed,) for many years before I came into possession of it. Let us look a moment into that axiom—the greatest profit comes out of the last cord of manure. With four cords of manure to the acre, on *good* soil, the average yield would be about four tons of Hubbard squashes; with six cords of manure, the average yield would be about six tons; with eight cords, the yield would be from seven to eight tons. These are real results, that I have had in my own experience. Here it will be seen that we gain about a ton of squashes with each extra cord of manure; in other words, by investing eight or ten dollars, we treble or quadruple our money in six month's time—quite a profitable bank of deposit is the manure heap! Not only is the crop heavier, but the squashes are larger, and, therefore, far more marketable, and, usually, at a higher figure, sometimes bringing $5 or $10 a ton advance in the market. Nor is this all; the virtues of the manure are not exhausted in the first season; the ground is left in higher condition for the crops of the next season. Again, let it be noted that the cost of cultivation of a poor crop is just as great as the cultivation of a large one, while the promise of a large crop is a great cheer amid the labor of caring for it. The strongest argument for the liberal manuring of this and all other crops is, that a certain portion of the crop but pays for the cost of producing it, and that the profits can only come *after* the cost of production is paid.

The cost of producing an acre of squashes, independent of the cost of the manure, will be:

Plowing twice	$6.00
Distributing Manure	3.00
Cultivating in Manure	3.00
Seed	4.00
Mixing Manure in Hills	2.00
Planting Seed	1.00
Three Cultivatings in course of season	5.25
Two Hoeings	3.00
Lime and Liming	1.50
Hand-weeding of large, scattered Weeds, after Runners have started off	1.00
Gathering of Crop into Heaps ready for Carting	2.00
Interest on Land	9.00
Wear and Tear, and Incidentals	2.00
Total, exclusive of Manure	$42.75
Add cost of four Cords of Manure, at $8.00, landed in Field	32.00
Cost of Guano, or some equivalent, to mix in Hills	5.00

Total cost of Crop when four Cords of Manure are used per Acre.$79.75

Now, as we stated above, the average yield of Hubbard squashes, under such manuring, would be about four tons. The average price of Hubbard squashes in the Boston markets, of late years, of such a size as four cords of manure to the acre would produce, has been about $20 per ton. At this rate, the returns (not deducting the cost of marketing) per acre would be $80, from which, deducting the cost of production, $79.75, we have 25 cents as the profits on the acre.

If, now, by adding two cords more of manure, or $16, to the cost of production, we obtain two tons more squashes, then the income is increased $40 (this supposes that we get but the same price per ton, but, in fact, I get from $5 to $10 more per ton for such squashes), and we have a profit of $24.25. The two cords of manure extra have more than doubled the profits; in other words, by adding about *one-six* to the cost of production, we double the profits.   Or, again, to give a commercial look to the matter, for every dollar invested in manure in May, in October, or five months, we receive a return of two dollars and a half.   The returns have proved in the same proportion up to eight cords, and at times up to ten cords, to the acre.   These statements are not visionary; they are drawn directly from *practical experience*, and can be corroborated by any farmer who has tried liberal manuring.   Catch a farmer of that class going backwards, and putting less and less manure on his grounds, what a phenomenon he would be !   No ; the progress of all enterprising farmers is in one direction.   By extra manuring the probabilities of receiving paying returns, are far greater in agricultural than in commercial life, as figures will readily show, though the popular belief is directly the contrary.

PREPARING AND APPLYING THE MANURE.

As a general rule in farming, the value of manures that are good for any crop, is increased by mixing them together, making a compost.   Ashes and lime are an exception to this rule; each, under certain circumstances, sets free the ammonia, (the most valuable portion of any manure,) and, being volatile, it escapes into the atmosphere.   In preparing a compost for squashes, the bottom of the heap may be made of muck that has been acted upon by the frost, sun, and rain of a year, if practicable; if this can not be done, let it at least be got out the fall previous, that it may be disintegrated, and, in a measure, sweetened by the winter's frost.   In the course of the winter, manure from the barn-yard may be hauled upon it. If this has been well worked by hogs, the better.   Toward spring, if night-soil can be poured into it, the richness of the heap will be much increased.   Sharp sand can now be thrown over the heap, and about as soon as frost breaks ground, the entire mass should be thrown over with forks, and thoroughly commingled, all coarse lumps broken up, and all frozen lumps brought to the outside of the pile. As soon as the mass begins to heat, the process should be repeated once or twice, until it is made as fine and as thoroughly mixed together, as time will allow. The sand will be found to be excellent to keep the manure finely divided and light, or to "cut" it, as farmers say.

In applying the manure for this or other crops, many farmers use all the manure in the hill; some, because having but little to use, they wish to get it as near the plants as possible, while others seem to hold the theory, that a circle of three or four feet in diameter is a sufficient area for the roots of squash vines to travel over in search of food. Where all the manure is used in the hill, the squash vines push over the ground rapidly, until just after the setting of the squashes, when they lose vigor, the squashes develop but slowly, and in the end there is a small crop of undersized squashes, for the roots, having meanwhile pushed beyond the hills, can not find food sufficient to sustain the growth of the vines. The roots of squash vines increase faster than is generally supposed. There is a theory that the roots grow to the same length as the vines, keeping pace with them in their growth. Whether the roots grow as long, or longer, than the vines, I can not say, but when the runner of a vine had pushed out but eighteen inches, I found the root over three feet in length, thus proving that at one period of growth, the root increases faster than the vine. This spreading of the roots through the soil is one of the marvels of vegetable life. I remember once lifting a small pile of litter that was about six inches deep, some dozen feet distant from a squash hill, when I saw what appeared to be a fine mist at the surface of the ground, but upon examination myriads of fine rootlets were seen, that were doubtless feeding on the decaying vegetable matter. Any person

who will examine a squash vine of the running sorts, after
it has set its fruit, will find roots pushed down into the
earth at each joint; and though these may be in part designed by the Creator to steady the vine, there can be but
little doubt but that they are designed also to feed the
long runners.   And this is proved by the fact, that if the
connection of the vine with the main root be severed,
while these subordinate roots remain uninjured, it will still
maintain a degree of vigor.   Such facts as these sweep
all theories of hill-manuring by the board, for if the roots
travel beyond the hill in search of food, there a wise cultivator will put food for them.   My usual practice is this:
to distribute all the manure from my compost heap over
the field, *after the first plowing, and before cultivating or
harrowing.*   This is thoroughly worked under (and but
just under) by the use of the wheel harrow or the
"Acme" harrow, both being modern implements, admirably adapted to the work, with the cultivator, aiming
to have everything as thoroughly fined up as possible.
After the manure is well worked under, the hills or drills
are marked off by dragging a chain over the surface, the
first line being made straight by setting up two poles
ahead, and keeping them in line while walking; afterward
the lines can be kept conveniently straight by carrying a
pole of the same length as the distance desired between
the hills, and using it occasionally as a guide.   After the
field is thus chained out in one direction, if it is decided
to plant in hills, it is crossed in the opposite direction,
the hills being marked out by the crossing of the lines
made by the chain.   If the surface is free from large
rocks, the hills can be marked out by running two sets
of furrows, the hills being made where they cross each
other at right angles.

In the hills I work in my manure, avoiding all stable
dung, or any animal manure, as this is liable to contain
seed, and to one who raises squashes for seed purposes,

this is quite a serious objection, for, in fact, I have found it almost impossible to keep squashes pure, where animal manure is used in the hill. I manure in the hill, or drill, with the most highly concentrated manures to be procured, such as guano, superphosphate of lime, or fish-guano. The reason for using highly stimulating manure in the hill is, to give the plants a quick start when young, that they may grow beyond injury from the ravages of the striped bug.

There is danger in using highly concentrated manures in the hill, that the roots of the young plants be destroyed —"burned" is the farmer's phrase; to prevent this, they should be most thoroughly stirred in with the soil. My practice is, to take such manure in a wooden bucket, and passing from hill to hill, scatter, if phosphates, as much as I can take up in a half closed hand; if Peruvian guano, about half as much, over a circle of about two feet in diameter. A man follows immediately after with a six-tined fork; he is directed to turn it just under the surface, and then draw his fork across the hill three times, and again three times at right angles with the first direction, ending with planting the fork in the middle of the hill, and giving it a twist around. I am thus particular in my directions, because day laborers seldom realize the corrosive effects of these highly concentrated fertilizers. After my man, a boy follows to plant the seed; he sweeps a circle with his finger around each hill, as he finishes planting.

After the vines have got so far along as to show their runners, I top dress the surface with hen manure, or some of the special manures above mentioned, and immediately follow with the cultivator.

It will be perceived that my system of manuring is based upon the theory that vines prefer their food near the surface of the ground. I draw this inference from the fact, that vines are great lovers of heat, being quite sensitive to changes of temperature, and also from tracing roots, and finding under the old system of deep manuring, that they would, at first starting, run but an inch or two below the surface of the earth, when they would spread out horizontally, and stretch on for some feet at a very uniform distance below the surface. Again, I find my crops very satisfactory under this system of manuring, and for a number of years have cultivated all my crop (four to seven acres annually), on this plan. My friends will note that I reduce my manure very fine, and mix it very thoroughly with the soil. My soil is a strong loam.

PREPARING THE HILLS.

The system almost universally advised and pursued in preparing the hills for planting, is to throw out the earth from within a circle of from two and a half to four feet in diameter, and from six inches to a foot in depth, oftentimes quarrying out rocks and digging into the hard-pan to get the standard depth. Then fill in with manure, and cover this with earth, raising a low mound in the form of a truncated cone about six inches above the surface. On this mound the seed are planted. Where the land is freshly turned sod, the hills are usually made by cutting a hole of the usual diameter in the sod with a sharp spade or axe. In my own practice, I have for years given up this method. The plan of excavating a hole, and putting in it all, or about all, the manure for the crop, appears to be founded on the theory that the roots will confine themselves to the area—an idea entirely erroneous, as we have already shown. Quarrying into the hard-pan and putting manure down to such cold depths, is inviting the vine to violate its instinctive love of heat. Again, this system involves a great deal of labor, particularly when sod land is planted, and on these latter the pieces of sod taken out of the hills remain nuisances over the surface of the field, either clogging the cultivator, or being knocked against the young vines. Let any farmer try the plan of preparing his hills as I have detailed above, and I will guarantee that he will not again return to the present system. If barn manure is to be used in the hills, let them be made saucer shape, broad and shallow. In preparing freshly broken sod, I find Share's harrow and the "Acme" and wheel harrows excellent implements, as they will pare down the sod to an inch in thickness, and make the soil as easy to be worked as old ground.

HOW FAR APART SHOULD WE HAVE THE HILLS, AND HOW MANY VINES SHALL WE LEAVE IN THE HILL?

The great error among farmers is to make their hills too near together, and leave too many vines in each hill. A very common distance for Marrow squashes is six feet apart each way, three or four vines being left in each hill.

A little figuring will show the bad policy of the practice. When a Marrow squash vine grows alone—and it oftentimes happens that one comes up among other crops on the farm—it will mature as many as three squashes, and at times half a dozen or more. Squashes so grown are almost always fine types of the particular variety. Now, on the contrary, when the hills are six feet apart, with three or four vines to a hill, the vines will not average *one* squash to each. I have been amused to receive the estimates of farmers of the number of squashes to the vine on the heaviest crop of Marrows they ever saw. As often as not the reply would be "three to the vine." Now an acre of ground planted 6 x 6 will have about 1200 hills to the acre; four vines to the hill would be 4800 vines to the acre. The present variety of Autumnal Marrow squashes as now grown, will average above seven pounds to the squash; if the vines produced on an average *one* squash apiece, we should then have 33,600 lbs., or over seventeen tons to the acre! Whereas the largest crop on record, as far as I am aware, of this variety of Marrow is less than eleven tons to the acre. From such figures the conclusion stands out with emphasis, that a system that, taking the average of crops, does not give over one squash to *two* vines, is unnatural, unfarmer-like, and un profitable.

The shortest distance, where the hill system of planting is pursued, should not be less than 8 feet each way for Boston Marrow squash and other running varieties, with the exception of the Hubbard, Turban, and Yoko-hama, which are ranker growers, and should not be planted nearer than nine or ten feet each way. The hills for the Mammoth varieties should be twelve or more feet apart each way. At these distances apart, two plants in each hill, (the vines being thinned down to that number when the runners begin to start), will be found sufficient to well cover the ground. Were it not for danger from the borer, I would never leave more than one vine to a bill,—putting the hills in each case proportionally nearer One of the finest crops of Turban squashes I ever raised, a crop that took the county premium for yield that year, was raised with but one vine to the hill, and the crop that took our county premium the year previous was grown with two vines to the hill. This brings us to the discussion of the Drill versus Hill system of planting. On the supposition that the great error in growing squashes has been to crowd the roots too much together below ground, while the vines were crowded too much together above ground, I have advocated, and to some extent practised, the Drill system of planting—having each vine entirely by itself, and distributing them evenly over the ground. Assuming that 10×10 or 100 square feet is sufficient room for the plant, on the Drill system, I allow 7×7 or about 50 feet for one plant. In planting on this system, the field is marked out as if for hills, the lines crossing each other every seven feet. In planting in drills I put three seeds along in the line, and when the plants begin to show runners, thin to one plant. By the drill system, in addition to the advantages above claimed, I think that the crop is more uniform in size, and the squashes are better proportioned in their forms than under the hill system. The vines being in a row, instead of a circle, the cultivator can be carried nearer to them. Most of my land is very uneven, otherwise I should always plant in drills in preference to hills.

PLANTING THE SEED.

The quantity of seed per acre for the Marrow and Hubbard varieties is set by practical farmers at two and a half pounds. This allows for liberal planting with a good surplus for after use, should cold or wet weather rot the seed, or insects destroy the plants that first appear. Four seeds in the hill and three in the drill is sufficient. The seed should not be put in, in the latitude of Boston, *earlier* than the 10th of May, and may be safely sown in ordinary seasons as late as the first of June, and success is sometimes attained with seed planted on rich, warm land as late as the twentieth of June. A part and sometimes all of the seed planted as early as the 10th of May will rot in the ground; yet to get the vines along early, and thus enable them to survive the attacks of the squash bugs, farmers oftentimes take this risk. If, after a cold, wet spell, the planter mistrusts the seed have rotted in the ground, let him scratch away the earth carefully with his fingers (it is infinitely easier to put a seed under than to find it again!), and if the seed is rotten, it will readily show it when pressed between the thumb and finger.

Seed may be planted either by using the hoe, (dropping the seed, and covering with the hoe,) or each one may be thrust into the ground with the thumb and finger. If the attempt is made to push the seed under by the finger alone, it is frequently left too near the surface, as the finger is very apt to slip by it unawares. If squir-

rels or field mice abound, it will be found safer to plant
with the hoe, as the little rascals appear to have a rare
faculty for smelling out the very spot where the seeds lie
when thrust under by the finger. I have known them to
begin at one end of a field and pass from hill to hill in a
straight line across the field, digging out every seed with
unerring accuracy. Seed opened with a knife and rubbed
with arsenic or strichnine and scattered in the paths will
generally check them. Two inches is ample depth in any
soil, and early in the spring, or in a rather wet or heavy
soil, the seed had better not be planted more than from
an inch to an inch and a half in depth.

Seed planted on upturned sod will vegetate sooner and
come up with larger rudimentary leaves than that planted
in rich, old ground; I presume that this is because sod
land lies lighter and is better drained and, consequently,
warmer than old ground. If, when the rudimentary
leaves appear, the seed shell adheres to either leaf, it
will do no harm, but if it confines both leaves together,
it should be removed, if it can be done without injury.
If a seed pushes but a single rudimentary leaf above the
surface, the plant rarely, if ever, comes to anything. If
these rudimentary leaves continue to increase in size, but
no leaf shows itself springing from between them, the
plant will come to nothing. If the young plants come
with a yellow color, it proves that the season is too cold
for them; if, on the other hand, they assume a very dark,
dull green color, it is usually because the manure with
which the young rootlets are in contact is too strong for
them; it is good policy, when the manure proves too
strong, to carefully remove some of the earth around the
plants with the finger, and with the finger stir in a little
fresh earth.

If, as at times will happen, some hills are entirely desti-
tute of plants, it is far better to plant them with seed
than to transplant surplus vines from other hills; true,

such vines sometimes root at once, but if checked in their growth by transplanting, they rarely amount to anything in the end.

This is one of the great conditions of success in squash culture, to *have the vines start well and make a rapid growth without a check.* Experience has frequently proved that late planted vines will oftentimes ripen their crops as early, and usually bear heavier crops, than those planted two or three weeks sooner.

HILL CULTURE AND LEVEL CULTURE.

After the plants appear, it is customary to draw earth around them; this is a good practice as far as it tends to keep them from being broken off by the winds. It is also an almost universal custom to draw up the earth into a mound of two or three feet in diameter, gradually increasing the height of it with each hoeing until it is six inches or more above the level of the field. I consider the labor entirely useless, to say the least, and have confined my own practice for several years past to level culture, making no hills, and drawing just earth enough home to each plant to keep it from being swayed, and thus injured by the wind.

HOEING AND CULTIVATING.

About as soon as the plants show themselves above the surface, the Cultivator should be set running. If the hills have been made equi-distant each way, the surface can be cultivated close home to them on every side, leaving but little work for the hoe. In no department of farming is the superiority of the Cultivator over the common hand-hoe brought out in stronger contrast, than in working the large open areas between squash hills. I

would rather have the work done by a one-horse Cultivator with a boy to direct the horse and a man to hold
the implement, than have the services of twenty men
with hand hoes; for not only would the surface be gone
over in equal time, but the ground be more deeply and
more thoroughly stirred, and the weeds be better shaken up
and turned under than would be possible with hoe culture. The cultivator should be used as often as the
weeds start, and whenever the surface appears hard, the
object being two-fold, to eradicate weeds and keep the
surface light and mellow. If witch grass abounds, the
Cultivator must be freely used, particularly when the
surface is hot and dry, that the vitality of the freshly
torn roots may be destroyed. It is not well to leave
the soil unstirred until the weeds have grown to some
size, as such are very apt to re-root. If the Cultivator
is used while the weeds are small, it can be spread
open to its utmost capacity. It is always well to have
one course of the Cultivator half overlap the preceding
one.

The last, and one of the most critical, periods when
the Cultivator is needed, is just previous to the push-
ing out of the runners over the surface of the field.
The vines are then growing rapidly, (I have found that
the large varieties, by actual measurement, grow as
much as fourteen inches in twenty-four hours), and if
special care is not exercised, the runners will push so far
as to prevent the final use of the Cultivator. The result will be a very weedy field the remainder of the
season. I have sometimes practised, when caught in
this way, breaking the hold of the tendrils and turning
aside with the hand such runners as had got so far
from the hills as to be in the way of the Cultivator;
but I have observed that where the tendrils are broken
from whatever they have naturally clung to, as often as
not the vines are injured so much by the wind that

they yield little or nothing; they are so twisted that they are often completely inverted; and though the leaf stalks are true to their instincts, and bring themselves perpendicular to the surface, yet in doing so, the curve they make, passing under the vine, lifts it a little above the surface, too far for the joint roots to strike into the earth to hold the plant in place and nourish it. It is a bad plan ever to break the hold of the tendrils, and as a general rule better allow the large weeds that appear towards the close of the season to remain, than to pull them up and tear them out from among the vines. If the weeds are to be removed, better cut them off close to the surface and leave them. A squash crop will foul the land at the very best, and let no one plant to squashes with the idea that the frequent cultivation allowed early in the season will tend to improve a piece of ground already foul with weeds; for young weeds will spring up as soon as the spread of the vines prevents the farther use of the Cultivator, and when the leaves begin to thin out, at the close of the season, under the stimulant of the sun and air, these soon become mammoths in the rich soil. When we consider that climbing appears to be natural to the squash vine, the injury caused by breaking the hold of the tendrils, and by the moving about among the thick net work of vines to do this, in connection with the fact that at best it is next to impossible to keep the ground in clean condition, I question whether, as a general rule, it is not better to allow these late and large weeds to remain untouched, and leave the clearing of the ground to the crop of the next year.

When the area of ground is small, and very clean culture is desirable, I would advise the driving of a few stakes among the vines to give the runners a hold when they first push out. It is not necessary that these stakes should protrude more than one or two inches above the surface.

Many old farmers lay down the rule that no one shall set foot on the squash patch after the vines meet between the rows. This is a good general rule, for most men tread among vines as ruthlessly as though passing among wire cables, crushing them under foot with perfect impunity. I don't think I ever saw a farmer pass among even his own vines with what I should call proper care. If necessary to pass among vines, carry a short stick in one hand to lift the leaves to see where the foot is to rest before planting it.

SQUASHES WITH OTHER CROPS.

In the vicinity of large cities, where land, manure, and labor are costly—and much of the market gardening in the vicinity of Boston, New York and Philadelphia is on land worth from $500 to $1,000 an acre—farmers usually grow their squashes in connection with other crops, such as Peas and early Cabbages or early Potatoes. If early Peas or Cabbages are planted in rows three feet apart, by omitting every third row, and planting this to squashes at the usual time, the crops will not interfere with each other, as the squashes do not push their runners till July, after the pea crop has been marketed. With Cabbage, the third row may be omitted, or every third plant in the third row; this will give the squashes 9×9. It will be seen that squashes can be raised only with the earliest varieties of Cabbage, such as Early Wakefield, Early Oxheart, Early York, Little Pixie, Burnels, King of Dwarfs, that have been started in a hot bed. The plan practised occasionally of growing squashes among corn, I consider a bad one. It is very common in the country to plant at the second hoeing a couple of seed of the Yellow Field Pumpkins in every third or fourth hill, and the yield is usually satisfactory to the farmer; though if a field was divided in two, and an accurate account kept of the income from each half, I am inclined to believe that it would be found that what was gained in pumpkin was more than lost in corn. Squashes are more delicate in their habits than the hardy, rough vined pumpkin, and the result of attempting to grow them with corn is usually a small crop of inferior specimens.

SETTING OF THE FRUIT.

Soon after the runners have put forth, blossom buds will begin to appear at the junction of the leaf-stalks with the vine. As the buds develop, the stems will develop also, until the latter grow a foot or more long, a little longer than the leaf-stalks. The blossom now opens, and we have a large yellow flower, several inches in diameter, with a powerful and rich fragrance, very similar to that of a magnolia. This flower has at the center a yellow cylinder, about an inch in length, covered with fine yellow pollen. I find that many persons look for their squashes from this class of flowers. Squash vines have the sexes distinct in each flower, being what botanists call monœcious. These are the male flowers, and from their structure can never produce squashes; their office is wholly to supply pollen to fertilize the pistillate or female flowers. The first pistillate or female blossom rarely appears nearer the root than the seventeenth leaf, or farther than the twenty-third. Instead of having a long stem to support it, this flower opens close down to the juncture of the leaf-stalk with the vine. It has a small globular formation beneath it, which is the embryo of the future squash. If the structure of the center of the blossom is examined, it will be found to differ from the tall, male flower, in having the central cylinder divided at the top into several parts, usually four, sometimes six in number. These are what botanists call the pistils, and it is necessary

2

that the fine yellow dust of the male flower should touch these, to fertilize them, that seed may be produced, and consequently a squash grow—for the *primary* reason why a squash grows, is, to protect and afford nutriment to the seed, the use of it as food being a secondary matter. This may be proved by so confining a blossom, that no pollen can get access to it, when the blossom will usually wilt, and the embryo squash turn yellow and decay. If the female flower be broken off from the embryo squash before the flower has come to full maturity, the squash will decay. These female blossoms are so covered and hidden by the tall leaves, that it is evident that the fertilizing pollen must be conveyed to them by the bees, to whom the squash field affords a remarkably rich harvest. All of the crossing or mixing of squashes is caused by the pollen from the male flowers of one variety being carried by the bees to the female flowers of another variety. SQUASHES ARE CROSSED OR MIXED IN THEIR SEED, AND NOT IN THE FRUIT. Many cultivators are in error on this point; they have the very common illustration of the crossing of different varieties of corn in their mind, where the mixture of the varieties is at once apparent to the eye, and infer from this, that the mixture between different varieties of squashes should make itself visible to the eye *the same season it occurs.* A moment's reflection will correct this; *the crossing of the first season is always in the seed,* and for this reason we see it in the corn the first season, as the seed is immediately visible to the eye, while the various colors of the different varieties also aid us in the matter. With squashes the crossing is likewise in the seed, and hence can not be seen in them, until the seeds are planted, when the yield will show the impurity of their blood. But, though the crossing can not be seen in the squashes themselves the first season, yet, if one of the varieties planted near each other, has seed having the peculiar, thick, salmon-colored coating, so characteristic of some of the South American varieties, this indication of admixture may be detected by the eye the first season. The parallelism between the crossing of squashes and corn may be carried further, for it is oftentimes true with corn as with squashes, that there is a mixing of varieties, of which no indication can be detected in the seed by the eye the first season, which a second season will develop—what was before an eight-rowed variety, into a ten or twelve-rowed sort, or dark kernels may be replaced with white ones, and by numerous similar freaks, bring to light an admixture of varieties.

It is of considerable practical importance, that the law of admixture should be clearly understood, that the risk, incidental to planting seed from squashes that *look* pure, should be generally known ; for it will be seen from what I have written, that seed taken from squashes that externally are perfect types of their kinds, may yield a patch, where every one may show marks of impurity. Again, no matter how many varieties are planted together, no crossing from the result of that planting will be seen in the *external shape, color, or appearance* of the crop *the same* season.

To have squash seed pure, the squashes from which they are taken, must have been grown isolated, and this not only one season, but for a succession of seasons. Should several varieties of squashes be grown together, and it be desirable to keep one variety pure, it can be done by preventing any male flowers of the other varieties from maturing—no easy job, as those who have tried it know. The product of any particular blossom may be kept pure under such circumstances by covering with fine muslin, removing it only to fertilize with pollen from a male flower of its own vine.

The location of the female blossom, in a measure covered by the leaves, and low down, but little affected by the wind, would render it probable that it depends for fertili-

zation on the bees, rather than on the wind; and the fact
(as a friend who has tested it, informs me) that if only a
high fence intervenes between two varieties, the admixture
between them is comparatively small, corroborates this
theory. To preserve the degree of purity that is necessary in raising different varieties, requires planting at distances apart varying with the natural aspect of the country; a level tract requires longer distances than would
be necessary in an undulating country, and a space inter-
vening abounding in flowers is a better protection
than an equal distance where flowers are less numerous.
The object is to get the pollen removed from the thighs
or bodies of the bees, or have it covered by the pollen of
other flowers, before they can pass from a field of one variety of squash to that of another.   My own practice is, to
secure the planting of one continuous district of country
with the same variety of squash, by giving to farmers,
whose lands are near my own, my stock seed for their own
planting.   Even with this precaution matters will have to
be looked after, lest after all promise to the contrary, greed
can not muster sufficient moral courage to induce them
to pull up the transient vines that spring up from the manure among potatoes or other crops. Old farmers will pro-
fess, from the appearance of the calyx end, to classify
squashes as male or female; this is all nonsense, for, as
will be inferred from what has been stated, every seed
from every squash contains the two sexes in itself, in its
capacity to produce both male and female flowers.

Squash fields usually make about three settings of fruit.
I do not mean by this that *each* vine makes three settings,
but that this is usually true of a field as a whole.   It often
happens, that most of one of their settings, usually the
second, turn yellow and rot, after many of the squashes
reach the size of goose eggs. This is very apt to take
place, should there be a cold, wet spell just after they
have set. Sometimes all three of the settings will grow,

and then stories of great crops will be heard of in the
squash districts.   When a young Hibbard squash is making a fine growth, it will have a shining green appearance,
as though just varnished,   If the appearance of the squash
changes to a dull green color, the days of that squash are
numbered; it will soon shrivel and decay.

PINCHING VINES.

I have seen a vine perfect the growth of a squash 20 lbs.
in weight, though it had been cut off within a foot of
the squash when it had reached the size of an orange, and
another squash of about the same size was also matured
on the same vine, about four feet nearer the root.   The
vine was highly manured, and grew on very deep and
rather moist muck and loam.   I can not yet determine the
laws which govern the art of pruning vines.   I have had
some, the young squashes of which appeared to do finely
after the extremities of the runners were nipped at near
the close of the season, and others, where the young
squashes turned yellow and died, under, seemingly, pre-
cisely the same circumstance.   I am inclined to think,
that it is not well to pinch off the ends of the vines before the young squashes have attained to the size of a
large orange.   How far a crop of squashes might be increased by the nipping of the vines, or a pruning of the
roots, is a problem yet to be settled.   The use of the
cultivator just before the vines spread, must do much
in the way of root-pruning the vines.

THE RIPENING AND GATHERING OF THE CROP.

In seasons, in which the early part of summer is cold,
farmers sometimes get almost discouraged with the small
number of squashes that set, and the slow growth of such

as do form, but a few hot weeks may entirely change the aspect of affairs.

When we have good corn weather, it takes but a few weeks to mature a squash. I have known instances when the first fruit set was completely destroyed by a hail storm, which occurred in September, and yet a fine crop of squashes was gathered from the vines. When June and July are colder than usual, farmers will often come out from an examination of their squash patch with a significant shake of the head, yet I have never known a season, in which cold or wet prevented the growing of a fair crop of squashes on land selected with judgment, well manured, and taken care of. The degree of ripening to which the crop attains, will be affected by a cold and wet season, but the chances of a crop are equally good with a season wetter and consequently colder than usual, as with a season hotter and dryer than ordinary, for, in addition · to the check to their development caused by a drought, the bugs are most numerous and active in a dry time.

Ripening is indicated in the soft or fleshy stemmed squashes, such as the Hubbard, Marrow, and Turban, by the drying of the stem, which shrinks just where it joins the squash, and a dead, punk-like appearance which it assumes. The leaves near the root gradually turn yellow and dry up, and the squashes themselves change color; the Hubbard assuming a duller, more russet color, and the Marrow and Turban sorts a deeper orange. The skin of the Marrow and Turban will now offer more resistance to the thumb-nail, while the Hubbard will begin to put on a shell, which will be first detected near the stem end. It is a singular fact, that the shell of the Hubbard squash usually begins to form on the under side—the part towards the ground. When this stage is reached, squashes can be safely cut for storage.

At some seasons, a large portion of the crop, and, at most seasons, a small portion of the crop, just before

ripening, are affected by a blight, which turns the leaves
black near the hills, when they die down, and all the signs
of early maturity are presented to the inexperienced eye.
When the process of ripening goes on naturally, the exposure to the sun's rays, after the leaves have died, does
no harm, but promotes the full maturing of the squash ;
but when squashes become exposed before the natural
time, by the blighting of the leaves, they are, particularly
if of the hard-shelled kinds, apt to be "sunscalt," as the
term is, by which is meant a bleaching, or whitening of
the part most exposed to the sun.   Such squashes rarely
form shells, and, if badly scalded, are apt to rot at the part
affected.   In cutting squashes from the vines, a large and
sharp knife is needed.   There are two ways to cut squashes
from the vines; one is, to cut the vine, leaving a small
piece attached to the stem.   By so doing, the stem does
not dry up so readily, and as large stems, when green, will
weigh as much as a quarter of a pound, if squashes are to
be sold soon after gathering, this makes considerable addition to their weight.   Narrow, selfish men sometimes cut
their squashes this way.

The usual way is, to cut the stem from the vine.   When
first cut, more or less sap will run out in a stream from
the hollow stem, though the squash may be fully ripe.

A CRITICAL PERIOD.

What shall be done with the squashes after they are cut
from the vines ?   The stems need a little exposure to the sun
to scar them, and the earth, which adheres to those grown
on low land, should be carefully rubbed off while moist,
as soon as the squashes are cut.   A good way to accomplish
this, is, to let the squash remain where it is cut, provided
the leaves do not shade it, care being taken to give it a
turn, to bring the under side up to the sun.

If there is danger from frost, it is better to gather them

together at convenient distances, that they may be more readily protected. The interval between the cutting of squashes and the storing of them is a critical period, as oftentimes the keeping of the crop depends upon the course then taken. There is a pernicious practice, quite prevalent, of placing them in piles as high as can be made, without their rolling off. Should frost threaten, this, of course, is necessary in order that the mass may be the more readily covered with vines to protect them; but when so piled, as soon as danger from frost is over, they should at once be taken down, so that all may be exposed as much as possible to the sun and air. Farmers, in handling squashes at this period, are apt to lose sight of one important fact, viz.: that when a squash is cut from the vine, its vitality is impaired, and it has no longer such power to resist the effects of atmospheric changes as it had previous to the separation. I say its vitality is "impaired," for the fact that the seed continues to fill out for a month or two after the squashes are gathered and stored, proves that there is a degree of vitality, however feeble, yet remaining in the squash after separation from the vine. The fact that sap exudes and gradually thickens into tears, or, at times, runs in a stream from the stems when cut, no matter how ripe a soft stemmed squash may appear to be, seems to prove that some vital function of the sap vessels has been disturbed; while the greater readiness with which such squashes decay, carries us beyond theory to the *fact* of a diminished vitality. I have known the lower layer of a lot of Marrow squashes in the field, to be found rotten through and through on removal— and this when there had been no frost to injure them—the result being due wholly to the dampness of the ground, during a rainy interval, acting on a diminished vitality.

I have known instances in which lots of Marrow squashes that had never been touched by frost, and were perfectly sound when stored, were suddenly covered with spots of black rot, soon after they were put into a dry apartment. These lots had been exposed in the field in piles during a series of days of cold rain. The practical lesson to be drawn from such facts is, that squashes should never be left in the fields exposed to cold rains after cutting.

After the stems have had the sun a couple of days to dry and sear them, and even before, if cold, wet storms threaten, the squashes should be piled with great care on spring wagons, and taken from the field. The rule should be laid down as invariable, that no squash shall be dropped in any stage of its progress, from the field to the market; they should always be *laid* down.

THE STORING OF THE CROP.

Squashes are usually at their lowest price in the fall of the year, after the crop has been gathered, and before the first severe frosts. The crop being bulky, and requiring dry storage, farmers are intent on getting it to market before cold weather sets in. After the first severe freezing weather, the crop is usually held at a higher figure, as the surplus not intended for storage has been disposed of. In the immediate vicinity of the large cities of the North, a large proportion of the crop is stored in buildings known as " squash-houses," to be marketed during the winter and spring months. These buildings are oftentimes old dwelling-houses, school-houses, or ware-houses, removed from their original locations to the farm, and then put to this secondary use. I present a vertical section of my own squash-house, by which the general features of all of them can be seen at a glance.

In dimensions, the building is about 24×35 feet, with a height of 10 feet to the plates. It is divided into three rows of bins, which are separated from each other and the sides of the building by aisles, (*A, A, A,*) about 26 inches in width, a distance which admits of the easy handling

2*

of a bushel basket, or barrel. The bins, (*B*, *B*, *B*,) are about 5 feet wide, 26 inches high, and $25^{1}/_{2}$ feet long. The uprights, which support the series of bins, are small joists, 2×4 inches, with cross-ties of inch or inch and a quarter board sunk into them, on which the several platforms are laid. These uprights are the width of the bins apart, viz.: $5\frac{1}{2}$ feet. At the edges of the bins, boards, 6 inches

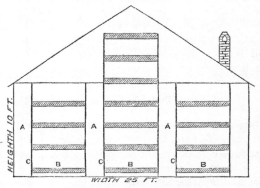

SECTION OF SQUASH-HOUSE.

wide, are laid, to prevent the squashes from rolling out. These boards should be planed on the inner, upper edge, that they may not cut into the squashes that lean upon them. The series of floors are made of strips of board, from four to six inches wide, nailed about half an inch apart, to allow a circulation of air. It is well to have the lower floor a sufficient distance from the floor of the squash-house, to permit a cat to go under. The cellar wall should be carried close up to the floor, by filling in front of the timbers with brick, or small stones and mortar; this will prevent rats from working through. As the building is designed to support much weight, it should be strongly braced by timbers crossing from plate timber to plate timber, to prevent spreading, while the cross-timbers, in the cellar, require props of masonry, or joist. To economize in fuel, on the two coldest sides, my squash-house is double plastered, and has double windows all around; some have inner wooden shutters to each window, which are kept up during cold weather, both day and night, only as much light being admitted, at times, as may be neces sary, while attending to work. The roof has five sliding windows, which assist in ventilation and give light to the upper part of the building, that otherwise would be quite dark when filled with squashes. The stove is at one of the coldest corners, with a funnel passing across to a chimney at the opposite corner. A building of the above proportions will hold about one ton of Hubbard squashes to two bins, and by careful and close stowage in all available room, it can be made to hold about sixty tons.

There is an advantage in having a low, wide building rather than a high and narrow one, as a greater portion of it is accessible from the floor, it is less exposed to cold winds, and the heat is more evenly distributed. In a high building, the heat in the upper portion is apt to be excessive.

The squashes should be brought to the squash-house in a dry condition, and be stored before dew falls. The stems being yet green, the squashes should be so piled as to bring these to the outside as much as possible. In placing the squashes on the shelves, put the largest ones on the bottom, giving them all a slant in one direction; they will thus pack better, and the uniformity will be agreeable to the eye. From the beginning of the storing, every window and door should be kept open during fair weather, and a fire at the same time will help in the drying of the stems. Should there come a damp time of one day or more, by all means start the fire. The stems will be apt to mould some, and the air of the building have a disagree· able smell if they decay, though a little moulding may always be expected. In about three weeks from the time of storing, the stems will be dry. In handling the squashes, I need hardly reiterate the caution of care. My practice is to form a string of boys, from the wagon to the shelves, and the squashes are tossed from one to another, with the caution to handle them like eggs. Boys well trained will not drop more than one squash to the ton, and I have known my boys to pass several tons without dropping a single squash.

CARE DURING THE WINTER.

If the squash-house has been built with reference to warmth, when once filled with squashes, it is surprising with what little fire frost can be kept out. The mass of squashes are, in themselves, a great store-house of heat, and with inside shutters for the coldest weather, the building is frost proof, with a small outlay of fuel.

In my own building, capable of storing sixty tons or more, I have a salamander stove of capacity sufficient to hold two hods of coal. In ordinary winter weather two hods of fresh, and a hod of sifted coal for night use, will last about twenty-four hours. To keep the fire over night, I leave the cover off about half an inch, and, if very windy, also put up the door in front within half an inch of closed. When I first attempted to keep squashes during the winter in very cold weather, I frequently sat up till midnight, and then retired with much anxiety, lest Jack Frost should steal a march on me before morning; but from experience I find that a salamander can be as well regulated and as readily controlled as a Magee stove, while the greater length of funnel that can be used with them, by reason of their superior draft, is a decided advantage.

No one can keep squashes to the best advantage, until he has fully learned to so control his fire as to keep the temperature near the freezing point, and yet not endanger the squashes. From a want of this knowledge, almost all squash-houses are kept at too high a temperature, and, as a consequence, the squashes lose in weight and quality, and, if they are Hubbards, in appearance also, losing their

fine dark green color, and becoming of a reddish, rusty hue.
The best temperature is as low as forty degrees. After
squashes are stored, the great desiderata are a low tem.
perature and a dry air. Should the weather be mild in the
course of the winter, never be tempted to open the windows *unless the air is dry,*—a very rare thing in winter,
as, on most mild winter days, the air is loaded with moisture. If it is desirable to air the squash-house, select a dry
day when not very cold, start up the fire and open the
windows at the roof. Squashes that were grown in a wet
season, will rot most in winter, and *vice versa.* Other
things equal, the keeping of squashes depends greatly on
the hygrometric state of the air—in other words, the
dryer the air the better they will keep. This is the reason
squashes keep better in a squash-house than in a cellar—
the house is no warmer than a cellar, but the air is dryer.
In dry, sandy cellars, by the aid of a fire, they can be kept
about as well as in a squash-house. Squashes in dry
cellars will usually keep very well until January, and sometimes to the first of February, particularly if the damp,
external air can be kept from them. Several years ago I
lost not far from twenty-five tons of squashes in about ten
days, as I now believe, from having admitted the warm,
damp air of a January thaw into the cellar. After squashes
are stored, the less they can be handled the better; and
in cellars, it is oftentimes better to let a few rot than to
overhaul squashes late in the season with reference to
culling out the rotten ones, for, after such overhauling,
they usually decay faster than before. Cellar-kept
squashes have some advantages over these kept in a squash-
house; they keep their original rich green color, lose but
little or none in weight, and are of better quality. They
do not keep as long, and, if the cellar was to any degree
damp, they quickly perish when sent late to market. This
fact is now generally known to dealers, and they hesitate
to purchase cellar-kept squashes late in winter. The win-

ter of 1866–7 was a memorable one among the squash
men of Massachusetts. Squashes being remarkably plenty
and cheap in the fall, every squash-house in the vicinity of
Boston was filled to overflowing. As the season advanced,
squashes began to show a remarkable tendency to rot, and
the result was that, in many cases, as large a proportion
as four-fifths of the crop rotted before spring opened. The
summer previous had been unusually wet and cold.

If apples, squashes, or any other fruits are gathered
ripe, the next step is to decay; but if they are not fully
ripe, they have this intermediate step to take before decaying. Heat is an agent in promoting progress in each
of these steps; hence, the less heat above a freezing temperature in which squashes can be kept, other conditions
being equal, the longer they will keep.

The very small squashes which are usually given to stock
as soon as gathered, are among the very best for keeping,
provided they are stored in the warmest part of the building. Late in spring they are salable at a high figure for
cooking purposes. Out of about five hundred pounds of
such squashes stored so near my salamander that the
outer tier cooked with the heat, I found but about ten
pounds of defective squash when I overhauled them
for the first time, near April. Squashes planted about the
first of June will usually keep better than those planted
earlier, on the same principle that the Roxbury Russet,
and Baldwin, keep better than the Porter, or Sweet Bough
apple, the former not being ripe when gathered. The
order in nature is that fruit shall ripen before it decays.

MARKETING THE CROP.

Squashes are sold by the squash, by the pound, and by
the barrel. Sales of the fall and winter varieties by the
squash are altogether unknown in the Eastern States, at
least so far as my knowledge extends. In the markets
of New England, after the summer squashes, of which

there is but a limited demand, the Marrow and Turban are brought to market, and, before frosty weather sets in, they are sold by the barrel or ton to the dealers.   Late in the fall the Hubbards begin to come to market, or if sold just after gathering, are rather forced on the market, the Marrow and Turban being usually recognized as the squashes for fall use.   During the winter, the supply from the squash-houses around Boston is mostly brought to market in barrels, and sold by the barrel without weighing.   This is poor practice, as there is often a number of pounds difference made by the thickness of the squash, its size, the packing, and the size of the barrel.   Such a system of marketing is apt to tempt to petty trickery.

A greater or less proportion of stored squashes will decay under the most favorable circumstances.   It is the policy of the squash grower to lose as little as possible in this way, and the custom of the markets of Boston usually allows a little latitude in this matter.   Hence, particularly as the season advances, one or more squashes that hav small rotten spots on them, are often packed in a barrel. The Hubbard is a very deceiving squash; it may be entirely rotten inside, and yet, to inexperienced eyes, appear perfectly sound without.   If the outside has white mould spots, looking like some of the concentric mosses, the squash is usually sound underneath the shell; but if these mould spots are greenish or yellow, it is usually soft rotten in a spot just beneath them.   If the shell at either end, (and the Hubbard usually begins to decay at the ends), has a watery look outside, the squash is usually considerably decayed underneath.   If the Hubbard is very light, it has usually the dry rot inside; if remarkably heavy, it is sometimes water-soaken and worthless.   If a squash, on being cut, proves to be water-soaken, a close examination will usually show some small opening, where, during some stage of its growth, the air or water found entrance.

FROST–BITTEN SQUASHES.

With the utmost care, squashes will at times get frost-bitten. The Marrows and Turbans show this by turning to a darker orange color on the injured part. If as much as one-half of a squash has been frozen, it is affected all through, and will certainly soon decay; the best disposition to make of such a squash is, to keep it very cool until it can be fed to the stock. If less than half has been frozen, before the sun shines on it, turn that side to the ground, excluding the light as much as possible; this will take out the frost and save it, if any remedy will, though such a squash is always unreliable property. Some years ago I had a load of Marrow squashes brought me, which had been stored in a barn during a cold spell, and the outer tiers had been frost-bitten. I separated the badly injured ones, putting them, frozen side down, in a dark cellar on the damp earth, and stored such as showed no signs of injury on the shelves. In a few days no signs of the trouble could be seen on those stored in the cellar, and they kept apparently as well as though they had never been injured, while those stored on the shelves soon rotted badly. The hard-shelled squashes are not as much injured by frost as are the Marrow and Turban; if the squash has a shell, the result will usually be the production of a dry rot under the shell as far as the injury extended, and no further. I have cut Hubbard squashes in February that had been frozen in November, for about five inches square of their surface, and found all the injury limited to this space.

MARKET PRICES OF SQUASHES.

Marrow squashes have varied in price in the markets of New England from $10 to $40 per ton; these variations are caused, for the most part, by the quantity brought to market, for, though equal areas may be planted, there may be all this difference, owing to effect of drouth, or the greater prevalence of insects in one season over another.

Prior to the war, the Marrow ruled in the market at from $15 to $20 per ton, and the Hubbard at from $20 to $25. The extremes of prices of the Turban and Hubbard have been from $20 to $50; the average having been nearly $34. These are the market rates just after the crop is gathered. As the season advances, prices have sometimes risen to 50, 60, 70, 80, and 100 dollars per ton, and occasional lots kept late into the spring, and sold by the barrel, have brought as high as $140 per ton. I once sold four tons for $400; yet so very poorly did the crop keep that winter, the profit would have been equally great had I sold at $25 per ton in the fall.

Squash-farming, on lands pushed well out into the ocean, has some advantages over inland farming. Neither the cabbage or turnip fly, nor the pea bug, squash bug, or any other destructive insect—the Colorado beetle excepted —is nearly as prevalent in such sections as just back from the coast, while the temperature being three or four degrees higher late in the fall, usually carries the crop through the first severe frost, and gives it the advantage of two or three weeks of the good ripening weather, which frequently precedes the severe frosts that usher in winter. I have known years when the maggots and bugs proved so destructive to the vines, a few miles from the coast, as to bring squashes up to $40 and $50 the ton, while at the sea side the crop was as large as usual, having received but little or no injury.

EXPORTING TO FOREIGN MARKETS.

Squashes cannot be raised successfully in the British Islands, although the average temperature there is higher than ours. That period of intense heat which we call our "corn weather," is unknown to the English, and hence they cannot succeed in the open ground with our hot-weather loving plants, such as beans, corn, melons, cucumbers, and squashes.

While in London in the year 1872, I found by inquiry at Covent Garden Market—the great market of the metropolis—that the squashes of our country were unknown to the market-men. I made arrangements to ship them a ton as an experiment. On returning home I prepared a description of our standard varieties, told the facts relative to their general use in this country, and gave instruction in the various ways of preparing them for the table, as simply cooked squash, and also in the form of puddings and pies.

In answer to my inquiry how the English people liked our American squashes, the reply came that my agent had no means of knowing, for, as far as he had been able to ascertain, the whole shipment had been bought up by shop-keepers to show as curiosities in their windows. Further correspondence developed the fact that if they could be sold in Covent Garden Market at a shilling (twenty-five cents) apiece, very likely a large business could be done in them. I shipped my squashes by way of Liverpool, and the transportation overland from that port to London cost as much as the freight across the Atlantic; this, in addition to the other expenses, would have so much reduced the profits that at twenty-five cents each the margin on squashes costing twenty dollars per ton in this country, would have been too small to make the business inviting. Now that we have direct communication by steamer with London, it would be wise for some enterprising Yankee to try the experiment again. I would advise the shipping of none but the hard-shelled varieties, and only the ripest of these, as the damp hold of a transatlantic steamer makes a very poor squash-house.

SQUASHES FOR STOCK.

When a large quantity of squashes is stored, there will always be more or less waste. If in a large town, many of the spotted squashes can be most profitably handled by cutting out the decayed portion, and marketing the squash at a reduced price. It has been my practice for years to dispose of many of my defective squashes in this way, and the sales of these are a fair index of the comparative popularity of the Autumnal Marrow, Turban, and Hubbard squashes, in a community where they have all been grown for years, and are well known. The sales of my market-man would average, late in the fall and in early winter, ten pounds of Hubbard and Turban to one pound of the Marrow, though he offered the Marrow at one-third the price of the Hubbard and Turban. After many trials I have found it next to impossible to dispose of the Marrow while having a stock of Hubbard and Turban, hence I have adopted the plan of feeding the former to my stock.

I have fed principally to horned cattle and pigs. The squashes should first have the seeds removed, as these tend to dry up milch cows, or, if fed to pigs, to cause them to urinate very freely. The Marrow should be fed to horned stock either in rather large pieces or in quite small ones, to prevent choking. The Hubbard should always be cut into pieces not less than three inches square, as the shell and the curved form of large pieces combined, are too much for the cattle to manage.

If squashes are abundant they may be fed very liberally, a bushel and more a day for each head ; the only danger to be guarded against is, that they may relax the animals too much. In value for milk purposes, they appear to combine the good qualities of the Mangold Wurtzel and the Carrot, both increasing the flow of milk and improving its quality. This is more particularly true of the

Hubbard and Turban varieties. For fattening purposes, the Hubbard is excellent, as might be anticipated from the large proportion of sugar which is developed in it at the approach of winter. I have known a cow to be fatted for the butcher on the Hubbard squash, used in connection with good English hay.

In feeding to pigs, it can be used raw, or boiled with meal, or meal and scraps. My usual practice has been to boil the squash in a Mott's boiler, about a barrel and a half at a time, adding a peck of beef or pork scraps, broken into small pieces, and stirring in sufficient meal to thicken it. When cooked, it should be cooled as soon as possible, as the squash is very apt to sour and make the mass thin and somewhat unpalatable to the animals. I have known a sow with young to be kept wholly on raw Hubbard squashes, and on her coming in to be in better condition than was desirable. When hogs are fed almost exclusively on them, squashes are apt to give the fat a yellow tinge.

Squashes might be raised for cattle among corn, as pumpkins are (they are better food for animals than pumpkins), though I have doubts of the profitableness of such double crops, where each makes its growth and matures at about the same time.

No doubt an improvement on this is, to omit every third row of corn, and give the vacant space to the squash hills. Among seed onions, I grow squashes with little or no apparent detriment to either ; but in this case the crops are planted and mature with more than a month's difference between them at each end of the season. Besides horned cattle and hogs, many horses, goats, poultry, and rabbits will eat squashes with avidity.

As to their comparative value as food for stock, each grower must strike the balance for himself—the facts being, that the yield is from one-fourth to one-third as great as carrots, and from one-fourth to one-fifth as great as mangolds, while they require but a fraction of the care in cultivation and gathering that either of these crops do.

A number of years ago, I made a somewhat careful test to determine the money value of squashes when fed to milch cows, considering the three points—their fattening properties and their effect on the quantity and quality of the milk. I found that the animals ate but little hay when fed freely on cut squash ; they gained markedly in flesh, their milk was richer, and the quantity much greater. The result of the experiment was, that when fed to milch cows, ripe squashes were worth, under the above three heads, half a cent a pound. Their worth for either fattening, milk, or butter alone, my experiment did not determine.

VARIETIES OF SQUASHES.

Owing to the great tendency in the varieties of the Cucurbitaceous Family to cross with each other, hybrids are very common. Seed planted the first season after the crossing has been made, will usually produce a greater crop than either of the parent kinds, and individual squashes will be superior in quality to either of the parents ; yet, as a rule, hybridization is not desirable, for after the first season, there may be a deterioration in the quality below the average of the parent kinds, while the mixed are not so marketable as the pure varieties.

Hubbard Squash.—I have traced the history of this squash back to about 1798, when the first specimen was brought into Marblehead by a market-man named Green, who lived in the vicinity of Boston. The person who, when a girl, ate of the first specimen, died recently, aged ninety-three years. She recalled the form, which is very much like the present one—turned up "like a Chinese shoe." It is now over thirty years since the variety was first brought to our notice by our old washer-

woman, named Hubbard ; and, to distinguish it from a
blue variety that we were then raising, we called it
"Ma'am Hubbard's Squash"; and when the seed became a commercial article, and it was necessary to give
it a fixed name, I called it the Hubbard squash.   If
I had been able at the time to forecast its present fame,
and had I foreseen that it would become the established
winter variety throughout the squash-growing region, I
might have bestowed some more ambitious name ; and
again I might not, for the old lady was faithful in her

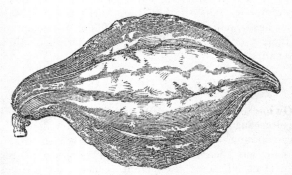

HUBBARD SQUASH.

narrow sphere to her day and generation—a good, humble
soul—and it pleases me to think that the name of such
an one has become famous.
   The form of the Hubbard is spherical at the middle,
gradually receding to a neck at the stem end, and to a
point, usually curved, at the calyx end, where it termi-
nates in a kind of button or an acorn.   In color it is dark
green, excepting where it rests on the earth, where it is of
an orange color.   It usually has streaks of dirty white,
beginning at the calyx end, where the ribs meet, and ex-
tending half or two-thirds way to the stem.   After the
squash ripens, the surface exposed to the sun turns to a

dirty brown color. The surface is often rather rough, presenting quite a knotty appearance. When the Hubbard is ripe, it has a shell, varying in thickness, from that of a cent to a Spanish dollar.

For a year or two after we began to cultivate the Hubbard, we cultivated also a blue-colored squash, called at the time the Middleton Blue. In a few years this squash became so thoroughly incorporated with the Hubbard, by repeated crossings, that it appeared to have the characteristics of a new variety ; hence we called it the Blue Hubbard, and for some years I spoke of two varieties of the Hubbard, a green and a blue kind. On testing the blue variety by itself, I found it had the characteristics of all hybrids—a tendency to sport. For this reason I have endeavored to throw it entirely out of cultivation in my seed stock.

After the Hubbard squash became somewhat noted, communications to the press occasionally appeared, claiming that it was but an old variety revived. After giving all of these many claims a fair examination, I am persuaded that the Hubbard is not an old variety revived, and that until it was sent out from Marblehead it was unknown in the United States. In my endeavors to trace its origin, the nearest I have come to it was in a variety of squash procured from one of the West India Islands, which had many characteristics in common with the Hubbard, though the shell of this squash was uniformly blue in color, and its quality was somewhat inferior.

Several claimed that it was but the Sweet Potato squash revived. I have myself raised a squash called by that name, and have seen two or more other lots that were raised by friends, from seed procured in different sections of the United States, and never have seen one that resembled the green Hubbard.

The apparent connection between the Sweet Potato and Hubbard squash has been made, I am convinced, through the blue variety, which, when without a shell, has a close resemblance to some of those kinds that go by the name of "Sweet Potato" squash.

American Turban Squash.—I have given the prefix American Turban Squash to distinguish it from the French Turban, with which many seedsmen have confounded it. The French Turban is the most beautiful in color, and the most worthless in quality, of all the varieties of squash that have come to

my notice. Nearly flat in shape, growing to weigh ten to twenty pounds, it has a large prominence at the calyx, shaped like a flattened acorn; this is elegantly quartered, with a button in the middle, and is most beautifully striped with white and a bright grass green, while a setting of bead-work surrounds it. The

AMERICAN TURBAN SQUASH. body of the squash is of the richest orange color. In quality the French Turban is coarse, watery, and insipid.

The American Turban is, without doubt, a combination of the Hubbard, Autumnal Marrow, Acorn, and French Turban, and the finest achievement that has as yet been obtained by hybridization. Like all hybrids, it tends to sport, and varies somewhat in quality, so that, while most of the squashes are of first quality, some will be found that are inferior. With such parents as the Hubbard, Acorn, and the Autumnal Marrow, we might expect to find a superior squash, and in the *average* quality of the Turban we shall not be disappointed; when fully ripened, it has dryness, fineness of grain, sweetness, delicacy of flavor, and richness of color. Like the Hubbard, it is edible before it is fully ripe; either of these varieties, particularly the Hubbard, being, when unripe, superior for table use to any of the varieties of Summer Squashes. The form of the American Turban is nearly cylindrical, the two diameters being usually in the proportion of three to five, while it is more or less flat at both the stem and calyx ends. At the calyx end there is usually a more or less prominent acorn. This may be very clearly defined, standing out quite prominently from the body of the squash, or it may be very much flattened and sunk within the body, with the outline barely traceable. In degree of prominence the acorn sports greatly, for, on squashes growing on the same vine, I have found, in one specimen, this part projecting very prominently, and fully developed, while on a second specimen it could only be traced in a very rudimentary form. It is not desirable that the acorn should be prominent, as the seeds extend into it ; at the calyx end of the squash, the meat is very thin, and, if the acorn is very prominent, a slight bruise will injure it, and cause the squash to rot. For this reason, I have of late years selected seed squashes from those specimens in which the acorn was not very prominently displayed, endeavoring to produce a type in which it should be little more than rudimentary.

Some writers on vegetables treat the American Turban squash as but an improved form of the French Turban, whereas it is a distinct variety. It is indebted to the French Turban for nothing more than the principal features of its form, getting its quality, keeping properties, color, and fineness of grain, from its other parents. As the American Turban is the result of hybridization, there is more or less variety in the shape and color of the crop; and this will continue to be so, unless, by long and close cultivation of a particular form, sufficient individuality shall be acquired by this one type to stamp the entire crop. Though it may be very pleasing to the eye to see every specimen alike, yet I consider it too great a

3

risk to cultivate a hybrid squash for this end ; for who knows what characteristics each parent has contributed, or how much these are affected by each other in combination ?   Until these points are determined, there is danger lest, in continued selections of a given type, some good traits should be eliminated.

We know that, in some way, the original excellence of the Autumnal Marrow squash has been lost, and no one can, with certainty, tell when or how this disappeared ; an admixture of other sorts was doubtless the first step towards this deterioration, and we are inclined to believe that a tendency to give prominence to some of the results of the first admixture, has gradually borne under the good traits of the original Marrow.

Autumnal Marrow Squash.—This is also known as the Boston Marrow, or Marrow, it having been a very prominent squash in the markets of Boston for a series of years.   A mongrel variety of it is also known as the " Cambridge Marrow."   This squash was introduced to the public by Mr. J. M. Ives, in the years 1831–2. When introduced, it was a small-sized squash, weighing five or six pounds, fine grained and dry, with an excellent flavor.   Market-men found that by crossing with the African and South American varieties, they could increase the size of the original Marrow ; they did this without troubling themselves about any risk of deterioration, and I doubt not that much of the present inferior quality of this variety is due to this vicious crossing.   In form the Marrow is much like the Hubbard, but with less distinctive prominence in the neck and calyx.   In color, the Marrow is between a lemon-yellow and a rich orange; the skin is covered with fine indentations, giving it a pock-marked appearance.   The body of the squash is divided into sections by slight depressions in its longest diameter.   Under the thin outer skin, or epidermis, is a thicker skin of a dark

orange color. The flesh is orange colored. The seeds
are somewhat larger and thicker than in the Hubbard,
and considerably larger, but not so thick as the Turban.
In quality the Marrow of to-day varies much; sometimes
we find specimens that are all that can be desired, particularly as we get near to the original type (this has
been kept more nearly correct in Marblehead than else-
where), but in its general character the Autumnal Marrow is watery, not sweet, and oftentimes deficient in
flavor and fineness of texture.   From its great productiveness, it is a favorite squash with market-men, and its

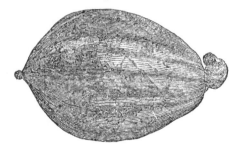

AUTUMNAL MARROW SQUASH.

rich orange color and handsome form render it popular
with those who have not become acquainted with the
more recently introduced and finer varieties.   There are
two varieties grown for the Boston market known as the
Cambridge Marrow.   One of these is quite large in size,
usually having the green color at the calyx, which indicates a mongrel variety; the other is of medium size, and
is characterized by a brilliant orange color which makes
it very attractive to the eye.   Both of them mature a
little earlier than the purer sort.

The Marblehead Squash.—Soon after I had introduced the Hubbard squash to the public, word came to
me that one of our old sea captains had it in his garden,

and had grown it there for several years, having originally brought the seed home with him from a foreign voyage. As I had endeavored in vain to trace the origin of the Hubbard, I was, of course, greatly interested, and at once called at the garden of the old gentleman. There I found a squash growing, which had a hard shell, like the Hubbard, but differing from it in the color of the shell, color of the meat, and in general shape, being quite a different squash. I procured some of the seed, and planted them in an isolated spot.

When the crop matured, I found, to my regret, that it was so terribly hybridized by an admixture with other

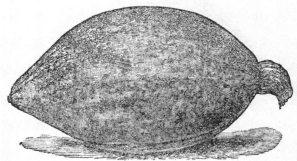

MARBLEHEAD SQUASH.

sorts of squashes (which had been grown year after year by the neighbors of the old captain), that it had lost its originality. I was therefore compelled to drop it, though very reluctantly, for the quality was remarkable.

Later I received a letter from an enterprising farmer in the West, who wished to send me a new squash, of the good quality of which he wrote in strong terms. I received the squash, cooked and tested it, found it surpassingly good, and became at once deeply interested in it. On further correspondence, I learned that the seed was originally brought from the seaboard, and that it had been kept perfectly pure. I obtained a supply of the seed, from which I raised a crop on my own grounds. I found that I had the old captain's squash over again, with the difference that now I had it perfectly pure! As the squash was first introduced to my notice in Marblehead, and was a nameless bairn, I concluded to call it after the old town "Marblehead"; and so we have the Marblehead Squash.

This new squash, as a rule, is characterized by a shell of a more flinty hardness than the Hubbard. It is usually thicker and flatter at the top. It has a greater specific gravity. The flesh is of rather a lighter color than the Hubbard, while its combination of sweetness, dryness, and delicious flavor is something really remarkable. In yield it about equals the Hubbard, while its keeping properties are declared to surpass that famous variety. In the important matter of purity, it excels the Hubbard, and every other squash that I have raised. Its outer color is a light blue, but it is not to be confounded with the blue-colored squashes that come at times from the Hubbard seed. If the seed of these mongrels be planted, their hybrid character will be seen by a terrible sporting, so dreaded by every farmer; while, on the contrary, the crop from the seed of the "Marblehead" will be found to excel in purity.

The Butman Squash.—This new squash is the only one of our running varieties known to have originated in the United States. For this fine variety the public are indebted to the scientific knowledge, the skill, care, and perseverance, of Clarendon Butman, Esq., of Maine. Mr. Butman selected for his experiment the Hubbard and the Yokohama, a variety from Japan, with the object of combining in one variety the best characteristics of both. Any one can make a cross between two varieties, and, in fact, nature is continually doing this through the agency of insects; but to combine the characteristics of the two squashes so thoroughly as to fix them, so that actually a new variety is produced with characteristics belonging only to itself, and fixed as permanently as in either of the parents, has been accomplished, to my knowledge, by but one man, and that man is Mr. Butman!

Mr. B. transferred the pollen of one variety to the other, with the precautions well known to every scientific man; and he repeated the process for two or three years, until he had achieved complete success. The new squash produced is, externally, very distinct in color from any

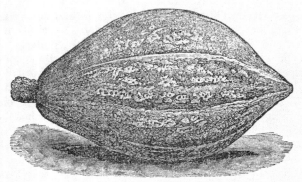

BUTMAN SQUASH.

other kind, being a bright grass-green, intermixed with white. In size and productiveness, it resembles the Hubbard; it has a thick shell and is thick meated. The color of the flesh is quite striking, being of a light salmon, and lemon color when cooked. It is very fine grained and smooth to the palate, and is remarkably dry, sweet, and delicious; it is entirely free from the pumpkin-like taste occasionally found in the Hubbard, and combines the flavor of that variety with the best quality of the Canada Crookneck. I am inclined to the opinion that the period when the Butman Squash is in its prime is from October to January, though as a keeper it is equal to the Hubbard.

Essex Hybrid Squash.—This is a cross between the Turban and the Hubbard, having the shape of the former and the shell of the latter. It is a very handsome looking squash, and the flesh is of rather darker average color than that of either the Hubbard or Turban. As might be inferred from its parentage, it is a squash of good qual-

ESSEX HYBRID SQUASH.

ity, though, in my experience, it is inferior to either a pure Hubbard or a pure Turban.

In the course of the past twenty-five years I have twice attempted to fix the type of the hard-shelled squashes which are occasionally found among the American Turbans, but have failed in each of the trials, succeeding, however, in each instance in getting about the same proportion of hard-shelled specimens as is found in the Essex Hybrid.

The six varieties of fleshy-stemmed squashes, described and illustrated in the preceding pages, include most of those raised for market purposes. There is a large number of other varieties, such as the Valparaiso, African, Honolulu, Sweet Potato, and others, some of which have quite distinct characteristics, that are more or less raised in the family garden; several of these are of inferior quality, some are hybrid, and though one or two may be desirable for the garden, yet none of them, as far as I have made acquaintance with them, have characteristics which would invite their general cultivation.

In that excellent work by my friend, Fearing Burr, "The Field and Garden Vegetables of America," will be found quite a list of summer, fall, and winter squashes. I am often in receipt of varieties of high local repute in different sections of the country, and it is possible that some of them when tested may prove worthy of general cultivation.

Passing to the hard or woody-stemmed varieties, we find included among them the Winter Crookneck, the Canada Crookneck, Yokohama, and several others.

The Crooknecks had their day and generation before the introduction of the soft-stemmed varieties. They were then the standard sorts, and the kitchens of thrifty

LARGE WINTER CROOKNECK SQUASH.

farmers were adorned with choice specimens suspended around the walls by strips of list, to be used during the winter, in the course of the spring, and even during the summer months. The Crooknecks are characterized by long, usually curved necks, terminating at the calyx end in a bulb-like prominence, which contains the seed. The vines are covered with rough spines, and in the shortness of their leaf-stalks, the smaller size and different color of the leaves, are readily distinguished from the soft-stemmed sorts. They vary much in color at the time of the gathering, and there is a tendency in all of them to change to a yellow hue in the course of the winter. In quality, the Large Winter Crookneck is coarse-grained and watery, while the Canada Crookneck is finer grained, and at times quite dry and sweet. The Winter Crookneck weighs from ten to twenty-five pounds and upwards, and the true Canada Crookneck, which is rarely found pure, averages from three to six pounds. In keeping properties the Crooknecks excel, frequently keeping in dry, warm apartments the year round, and, in a few instances, two years. When kept into the summer the seeds are at times found to have sprouted within the squash.

The Crooknecks are subject to a kind of dry rot, particularly in spring, which gives them a peculiar appearance when cut, the tissue between the cells having a dull, white color, though the fibres of flesh still retain their bright yellow hue. When in this condition they are worthless for table use. The true length of time in which a squash keeps, is that in which it retains its quality, and not its mere structure.

The Yokohama is from Japan, it having been received in this country, in the year 1860, by Mr. James Hogg, from his brother, then residing at Yokohama, in Japan. The vine is a very free grower and a good yielder, though, from the comparatively small size of the squash, the weight of the crop is not large, when compared with the Hubbard, Turban, or Marrow. The Yokohama is quite flat with somewhat of a depression at each end. The diameters are to each other as about one to three or four. It is deeply ribbed, and the flesh, which is of a lemon color, is remarkably thick, making it one of the heaviest of all squashes in proportion to its size. The flesh is very fine-grained, smooth to the taste, and has a flavor resembling the Crookneck. With those who like the taste of the Crookneck, the Yokohama will probably be very popular.

Externally, before ripening, it is of an intensely dark green, and covered with blisters, like a toad's back ; as

it ripens, it begins to turn a light brown color at both the stem and blossom ends, and, after storing, it soon becomes entirely a copper-like color, and is covered with a slight bloom. It may be well to start the seeds under glass, on squares of turf, though, after an experience of several seasons, I am persuaded that it is becoming ac-

YOKOHAMA SQUASH.

climated; indeed, my crop has of late years ripened with the Hubbard and Turban. The cultivation of the Yokohama is mostly confined, as yet, to private gardens.

Para, or Polk Squash.—This is a half-bush squash. In the first stages of its growth it has a bush habit, and sets its first fruit like a bush squash, but later it pushes out runners eight or ten feet in length, and bears fruit

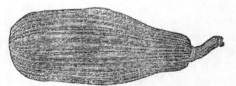

PARA, OR POLK SQUASH.

along them. The squash was brought to this country from Para, in South America. In shape it is oblong ; it is ribbed, of a tea-green color, excepting the portion which rests on the ground, which is of a rich orange color. The squashes weigh about three pounds each. They require the whole season to mature, and, when in good condition, the flesh is dry and of a rich flavor.

Like the Yokohama, I apprehend this will be very popular with a class rather than with the community at large. Both the Yokohama and the Para can be kept well into the winter. I have kept a Yokohama, crossed on the Turban, fourteen months, and Hubbards, in two instances, twelve months.

CASHAW SQUASH.

Cashaw.—This is the name given to a squash grown in the South, which in form, size, and general appearance, closely resembles the variety of Crookneck known in the North as the Puritan squash. In quality it appears to be of a coarser grain than are the Northern Crooknecks. It matures too late for the North, unless started in a cold frame. The seeds are peculiar in being surrounded by a thin fringe, which makes them of mammoth proportions.

Cocoanut Squash.—A magnificent little squash for table use, very prolific, yielding from six to a dozen or more to the vine. In beauty it excels every other variety of squash; indeed, specimens very naturally find a place on the mantel-piece as ornaments to the parlor— not being surpassed in beauty by any of the gourd family. The color is an admixture of cream and orange, the latter color predominating in the depressions between the ribs ; while the bottom, over a circle of two or three inches in diameter, is of a rich grass-green. The flesh is fine-grained, sweet, and very solid (the squash being remarkably heavy for its size), and the quality excellent, some-

COCOANUT SQUASH.

what resembling Canada Crookneck in flavor, but in every way superior.

Perfect Gem Squash.—I am well pleased with this squash. It is certainly what is claimed for it—an important addition to our list of squashes. In its habit of

PERFECT GEM SQUASH.

growth it is like the Cocoanut, and is very productive, as many as twenty-four squashes having been grown on a single vine.

The squashes are from four to six inches in diameter, of a light straw color, slightly ribbed, and have a thin, smooth skin. The flesh is dry and fine grained until late in the fall, when it is less dry and remarkably sweet. It is proving a good keeper as a winter squash. It ripens about the same time as the Hubbard. This variety deserves a place in every kitchen garden.

THE SUMMER SQUASHES.

The remarks made relative to the cultivation of the fall and winter varieties, will apply to the cultivation of the summer squashes, with the exception of the distance between the hills; this, as they are of a bushy habit, should be about five feet. In quality, the summer squashes have but little to recommend them; it is principally their fresh, new taste that makes them acceptable for the table. If my friends will use a half-grown Hubbard on their tables, in place of these summer varieties, they will find it far preferable. South of New York the cultivation of squashes is confined almost wholly to the bush varieties. Until recently, the New York market for fall and winter squashes has been largely supplied by the growers around Boston.

I find that there is a strong belief among prominent seedsmen in the Middle States, that the running varieties of squashes will not succeed in their section—they will not form the thick, fleshy root, they say. We, in the North, have always looked upon the squash as a half tropical fruit, and anticipated finding greater and greater success in its cultivation the farther South it was planted. It has all the characteristics of a semi-tropical plant, like the tomato and the melon, and should it be true that there is such a climatic limitation, it would be a marked exception to a general law. I have but little doubt that, under proper culture in the South, our running varieties would do as well as at the North. It occurs to me at this moment that the late Dr. Phillips, the former editor of the "Southern Farmer," stated to me, in the course of correspondence, that he had raised them by the acre in Mississippi, with complete success.

The standard Summer Varieties are the Yellow and White Bush Scollop, often called Pattypan or Cymlins (at the South), and the Summer Crookneck. Of these

the last named is the best.   All form a shell as they
ripen, and are then unfit for the table.   They should not
be cooked after the shell can be felt by the thumb-nail.
The Green-Striped Bergen is an early variety, quite popular in the markets of New York.   Several of the varie-

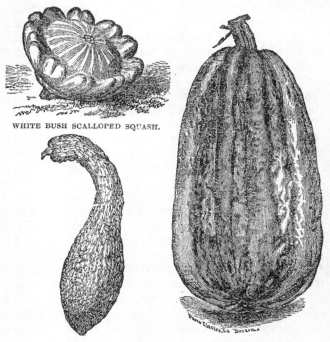

WHITE BUSH SCALLOPED SQUASH.

SUMMER CROOKNECK SQUASH.   CUSTARD SQUASH.

ties that are grown as gourds, for ornamental purposes,
are edible; a large proportion of them, indeed, as I
have found on testing the largest of my specimens
before feeding to the pigs.   As a general rule, all that
are not bitter to the taste are edible.

The Vegetable Marrow is about the only variety of

the squash family cultivated by our English cousins. With them it is brought to the table in the same style as our own varieties, or so cooked as to form part of a soup.

A friend who resided some years in England, informed me that one of the greatest novelties to an English eye was an Autumnal Marrow Squash, which he kept as a center-piece on his marble table for a month or more.

The Custard Squash is one of the hard-stemmed sorts, of a yellowish cream-color, oblong in shape, deeply ribbed, weighing from twelve to twenty pounds. It is quite a favorite. The flesh is fine grained and of a light straw color. The flavor is rather peculiar, and much liked in pies by some persons. This is a large variety, and appears to be allied in form, quality, and productiveness to the Pumpkins.

ENEMIES OF THE VINE.

The insect enemies are the Striped-bug (*Galeruca vittata*), the Pumpkin-bug (*Coreus tristis*), and the insect that produces the Squash-maggot. The Striped-bug appears about the first of June, and, several broods being hatched in the course of the summer, they continue their depredations throughout the season. After the vines have pushed their runners two or three feet, their vigor is such that the after depredations of this little insect are of no practical importance—with the exception of injury occasionally done to immature squashes, the upper surfaces of which are sometimes found covered with them, and hundreds of little cell-like holes are eaten out. The injury done by the Striped-bug is mostly confined to the period in the growth of the vine between its first appearance above the ground and the formation of the fifth leaf. They feed on both the under and upper surfaces of the leaf, and, sucking its juices, soon reduce it to a dry, dead net-work. The eating of the seed-leaves of the plant (the two leaves which first appear) is not always fatal, provided the bud that starts from between them is uninjured; if this, however, is eaten out, the plant is destroyed for all practical purposes, and should be pulled up and thrown away, even if the seed-leaves are wholly uninjured. In localities where the Striped-bug is not very prevalent, the greatest harm of its ravages is sometimes prevented by planting the seed about the 10th of May, should the weather permit, which will enable the vines to get so far advanced as usually to be beyond the reach of serious injury. The preventives to the ravages of this little insect, which attacks the whole Squash family, including cucumbers and melons, are numerous. They may nearly all be brought under two classes : those which act mechanically, by covering the leaves so as to make them inaccessible to its punctures, and those which repel the insect by their disagreeable odors or pungent flavor. The best protectors of the first class are hand-glasses, little frame-works covered with millinet or very coarse cotton cloth; or, as this insect flies but a few inches above the surface of the earth, any box, circular or square, having sides about ten inches high, from which the bottom has been removed, may be used. The remedies of the second class are those which are principally relied on where squashes are cultivated on a large scale. These should be applied early in the morning, when the dew is on, or directly after a rain, while the leaves are wet, that they may adhere. In using them a small fine sieve will be found very convenient. The best of these remedies I name in the order of their popularity in the squash-growing districts. Ground plaster, oyster-shell lime, air-slaked lime, ashes, soot, charcoal dust, and common dust. Probably the application of Paris green, either dry or in a liquid form, would prove as efficacious in protecting

vines from their insect enemies as it has in protecting the
potato from the attacks of the Colorado beetle. Plaster
and oyster-shell lime, I consider of equal value, and the
use of protectors in my grounds is confined to one or
other of these. Against air-slaked lime, which is very
commonly used, there is this serious objection : however
thoroughly it may be air-slaked, it still remains sufficiently caustic in its nature to seriously injure the leaves,
causing more harm, by its burning properties, than good
by preventing the ravages of the bug. I have seen an
acre of thrifty vines entirely destroyed, through the
caustic properties developed in the lime, by a gentle
shower that fell just after its application ; the leaves
were so burned that they rubbed to dust in the fingers.
Charcoal dust and soot not only protect the vines, but
serve also to draw the heat of the sun, oftentimes very
grateful to the young vines in the early season of the
year; while soot and ashes in all localities, and plaster
and lime in some places, as they are washed from
the leaves by the rain, serve as stimulating manures
to the young plants. The advantages of plaster and
oyster-shell lime are, that being very finely powdered,
they can be easily dusted over the vines, and their
conspicuous white color allows it to be seen at a glance
whether or not the leaves are fully covered. Common
dust as a protector sounds cheap, but the trouble of
collecting and separating the stones, that might otherwise injure the leaves, is more than an offset to the
cost of other articles. These protectors should be applied as soon as the young plant breaks ground, before
it has fairly shaken off the shell of the seed, as the insect
is then often at work, and the application should be re-
newed after every shower, the object being to keep every
leaf entirely covered, as far as practicable, until the fifth
leaf is developed. At this time the plants will usually be
beyond reach of injury from this little enemy, provided

the hills have been supplied with sufficient rich manure
to give them a rapid growth.   Among this class of remedies are, a decoction of tobacco and kerosene oil; a very
little of the oil (the proper quantity to be ascertained by
experiment) is added to water, which is to be stirred while
being applied. The application of water in which hen-manure, or guano has been dissolved, sprinkling the leaves
with a mixture of wheaten flour and red pepper, or snuff,
or sulphur, etc., etc., have been found efficacious by various persons.   Dr. Harris states that these insects fly by
night as well as by day, and are attracted by the light of
burning splinters of pine knots or of staves of tar barrels.
As insects breathe through pores in their bodies, such
strong ammoniacal odors as are given off from a liquid
in which hen-manure, guano, or kerosene has been mixed, must tend to suffocate and repel them.

As new land is much less infested with bugs than old
land, it will be better in sections where these insects are
very troublesome, to break up sward to plant upon.

In fighting insect pests, where but few hills are cultivated, pieces of board or shingle laid around the young
plants, just above the surface of the ground, will collect
many on their undersides overnight; on examining the
boards early in the morning, many bugs can be brushed
off into hot water or be crushed.   I don't think much
of the plan of killing them about the vines ; the old saying that "when one is killed fifty will come to its fu-
neral " appears to have a savor of truth in it, for I have
noted that when I have killed them near the vines there
seemed to be no end to the business; after constant atten-
tion, the bugs appeared to be about as numerous as at first.
I think that the odor from the dead ones attracts others.

The large black bug I consider rather a Pumpkin
than a Squash-bug.   In this and in other sections,
as far as my knowledge extends, where the cultivation
of the pumpkin has been given up for a number of

years, it has almost entirely disappeared. Occasionally
a leaf of a vine will be seen pretty well covered with
the rascals late in the season, but so scarce are they,
that for several years past I have not seen, on an average, more than one each season on my vines, and I cultivate several acres annually. When the plants are young,
they are likely to be found, if at all, below the elementary
leaves, sucking out the juices from the vine itself. For
these fellows there is nothing like finger work. I have
known an instance in the interior where they were so numerous on pumpkin vines planted among corn, that the
mere smell of them acted as an emetic to three separate
sets of hands that attempted to hoe the corn patch.

The Squash-maggot is hatched from the egg of an insect bearing a close resemblance to the lady-bug, but of a
size considerably larger. The eggs are usually deposited
near the root of the vine, within an inch or two of the
ground ; and in seasons when this insect abounds, eggs
are deposited at the junction of the leaf-stalks with the
stem, along some six or eight feet of vine. As soon as
the egg is hatched, the maggot begins to eat its way
through the center of the vine, and its borings will be
seen outside its hole, like those of an apple-tree borer.
The vines thus attacked will wither under a mid-day sun,
and the injured ones are thus readily detected. Squashes
on such vines usually make but little growth, and the
plants ultimately die. If the presence of the borer is early
detected, it can sometimes be killed by thrusting a wire
or stout straw into its hole ; sometimes the vine is slit
open, and the intruder found and killed ; but vines thus
treated do not always recover. If the slit portion is covered with earth and pegged down, sometimes but little
injury is done. I have taken thirteen borers from a
single vine, some of the largest being an eighth of an
inch in diameter and an inch in length.

It happens at times, after the vines have made a vigorous growth of several feet, that they suddenly wilt and die without any evident cause ; no insects are to be found on the leaves, there are no borers in the vines.   I am at a loss to explain the cause of this, unless it be that the vine has been poisoned by something that it has taken into its circulation.   I have picked half-grown plums that tasted as salt as brine.   The tree had received a heavy manuring with salt, and ultimately died, proving that there is such a thing in the vegetable world as a tree poisoning itself by feeding to excess on one variety of food ; and what is true of a tree may be true of a vine.

WOODCHUCKS AND MUSKRATS.

On low land, near water-courses, Muskrats will occasionally make sad havoc with the growing fruit ; while on uplands, the Woodchuck is sometimes exceedingly destructive.   If the portion troubled by muskrats is of small area, the squashes can be protected by taking boxes of sufficient size, cutting a narrow slit in their sides, and setting the fruit in them, having the vines enter and go out of the narrow slits.   When muskrats begin on a squash, so far as I have observed, they make a finish of it before injuring others.

Woodchucks are exceedingly destructive ; they rarely devour a squash entirely, but gnaw more or less all in the vicinity of their burrows.   If these burrows are not conveniently near the squash patch, they will leave the old, and make new ones close by, or even in the midst of the squash field.   The wounds made by their broad teeth soon heal, if the squashes have not reached their growth, and the gnawing has not been through the squash, but the crop is much injured for market purposes.   I have had a ton injured in this way, in one season, by a single woodchuck.   Singular as it may seem, I have noticed that squashes so gnawed, when the wounds are not very

deep, and have had time to heal over, will keep better
after being stored, than the average of the crop. A thou-
sand and one ways are given to catch and destroy the
woodchucks; traps set a little way down in their holes,
and carefully hidden with earth, and apples, containing
arsenic, rolled into their burrows, are among those that
have proved successful. It is worth while to offer five
dollars for the skin of a woodchuck that has commenced
depredations in a squash field.

SAVING SEED.

In selecting squashes for stock seed, take (while the
squashes are in the field, or immediately after they are
gathered) neither the largest nor the smallest specimens.
The largest specimens are very tempting, particularly so
if they have the true form, appear to be well ripened,
and, if Hubbards, have a hard shell; but experience has
proved that these, as a class, are most likely to be of im-
pure blood. Several years ago two of my neighbors, who
had become famous for their large Hubbard squashes,
came to me to get a new stock of seed to start from.
They stated that within a few years a large proportion of
their squashes had grown soft-shelled. As they had made
it a rule to select the largest specimens for seed, I have no
doubt that the admixture (which was very evident from
the loss of the hard shell characteristic of the true Hubbard) had crept in in that way. Every old squash-grower
is aware of the great change that has come over the Autumnal Marrow squash. When introduced, it was of
small size, weighing about five or six pounds, exceedingly
dry, fine grained, and rich flavored. Now its quality is
uncertain, for the most part greatly deteriorated below
the original standard, but *it grows to double the average
size* of the original squash. I have not the slightest
doubt that this deterioration is due to the vicious practice

of saving seed stock from the largest of the entire crop, these specimens deriving their extra size from larger and coarser varieties of the African and South American type. If any one has doubts of this theory, he can easily satisfy himself by examining the calyx end of a crop of the largest-sized variety of Marrow squashes, when he will find a proportion of them with the green color stolen from the African or South American family.

Having decided on medium-sized specimens for seed stock, select those that are most strongly marked externally with the characteristics of the variety. If a Hubbard, it should be very thick and hard-shelled, of a dark green color. Let it have a good neck and calyx end, and be as heavy in proportion to its size as possible. The stem of both this and the Marrow squash should stand at quite an angle with the fruit, and have a depression where it joins, as this indicates an early-ripened specimen. The flesh should be hard, fine grained, and thick, and not stringy on the inside. See to it that the squash swells out to a fair degree in the middle, and has an average proportion of seed. Having selected such specimens as these, bring them to the final test of the dinner-table, and reject every one that does not there show all the characteristics of dryness, flavor, and fineness that belong to a first-rate specimen.

I know that the injunction to select specimens that swell out to a fair degree in the middle is contrary to the course pursued by most farmers; yet I advise it on the ground that such squashes, having a good quantity of seed, have superior vitality and individuality, and being nearer nature's ideal of perfection in the animal and vegetable kingdom, are better able to maintain the species.

I have seen the working of this law most conspicuously in the Crookneck family of squashes. The cultivator's type of a fine market squash is one with as large a neck and as small a seed end as possible. Following out this idea, they select for seed, specimens with a small seed end, and the result, as far as I have observed, has been that the squash in the course of a few years has deteriorated and become worthless.

When to Take Out the Seed.—We have advised that the specimens for seed purposes be selected early in the season, because later, particularly when they have been exposed to a high degree of heat, the color becomes so changed that the work of selection becomes far more difficult. The next question to discuss is, when shall we seed them ? Contrary to the generally received opinion, the seed is not ripe when the squash is —in other words, though the squash has completed its growth, the vines dying naturally and the stem being dead and hardened, yet the seeds do not fully mature until some time after the squash is stored. The length of time will vary with the season, it being longer in a wet season and shorter in a dry one, the two extremes being from one to three months. Though seeds taken out as soon as the squash is gathered, may at the time present a very plump appearance, yet, if they are examined after they are dry, a large proportion will be found to be plump only on one side, most of them will be twisted, and not a few of them entirely wanting in meat. When seeding large lots for market, I have found the percentage of loss in the weight of the seed quite an important matter, it being as high as one-fifth. After the squash is gathered, the process of ripening the seed goes on until the entrails are absorbed, or taken up by the seeds, and the seeds continue to increase in plumpness and weight until the entrails are so far consumed that only so much remains as is necessary to hold together the seed structure. This final ripeness is indicated by the seed compartments in the squash becoming distinct, and the attachments peeling off like the skin from an orange. If,

when the squash is opened, the seeds are embedded in a
hard, dense mass of growth within, that does not readily
separate from the squash, they will be twice as hard to
clean, and when cleaned will weigh full twenty per cent.
short of the weight of well ripened seed.

The seed is cleaned from the refuse by being either
squeezed out or washed out. The best way to clean seed on
a large scale is, to crowd it through very coarse sieves into
tubs, most of the entrails being left behind, caught in the
meshes of the sieves; then, putting it into a revolving
churn with water, give it a thorough shaking up, and removing it into sieves for draining, dash over some clean
water, after which spread it to dry. If squeezed out, seed
will dry sooner, and when rubbed and winnowed when
dry will have a more velvety look than when washed;
but to get such seed clean requires a good deal of work.
The best way is to trample on it while it is tied up in a
strong bag, and follow this by rubbing between the
hands and in a sieve, finishing with a careful hand pick-
ing. Where a large quantity is to be handled, it is cleaned more quickly by washing than by squeezing out, but it
requires to be dried upon a comparatively clean surface,
whereas squeezed seed can be dried upon any surface,
no matter how dirty, as the refuse squash that remains
adhering to it effectually protects it from all injury.
Washed seed should not be spread more than one deep,
and squeezed seed not over one and a half deep; each
should be stirred after the second day. If washed seed is
stirred earlier, it is apt to be injured by the tearing of the
epidermis, which for the first day or two adheres strongly
to the surface on which it is spread. The temperature for
drying seed should not be over about one hundred degrees,
and better less than more. Never dry seed in an oven,
or very near a stove. The upper shelf of a kitchen closet,
or a plate on the mantel-piece, not too near the stove
funnel, are each of them handy, though housewives will

sometimes say they are not suitable places—if mice are apt to gnaw the seed in the closet, or children to see them on the mantel, for a certainty I will not dispute them.   When the quantity to be cleaned is small, the sooner it is attended to, after the entrails have been removed from the squash, the brighter the seed will look ; but if the quantity is large, by letting the mass stand one or two days, until fermentation begins and the entrails are partly decayed, the seed can be cleaned with far greater expedition.   Much care and some experience are requisite to determine how far fermentation can be allowed to advance.   As a general rule, if, on thrusting the hand into the middle of the mass, it feels milk warm, it should be at once mixed well together and the whole be washed out within six hours.   The great danger in permitting fermentation to advance too far, is in losing the white, ivory-like epidermis of the seed, thus destroying much of their beauty, and lowering their value for market purposes.   In washing the seed, the water used may be made about milk warm, and, as soon as they have been squeezed out of the entrails, skim them off the surface, dropping them into a sieve about as coarse as a common coal sieve ; when this is nearly full, dash over them a couple of buckets of water, giving them immediately a quick shaking, which will tend to work out through the meshes the fragments of entrails that were taken out with them.   If the hand is thrust into a mass of freshly washed seed it will collect a good many pieces of the entrails.   After pouring the water on the seed, incline the sieve at a sharp angle, in order that it may drain off. After they are well drained, pour them out on a large piece of soft cotton cloth, and rub and roll them well, to absorb as much of the moisture as possible.   Then spread as above directed.

When is Squash Seed Sufficiently Dry ?—It took me a couple of years to learn a very simple rule by which

4

this can be infallibly determined. Meanwhile I suffered a great deal of anxiety, took a great deal of extra care (I got out twenty-six hundred pounds of squash seed one season), and yet after all had a feeling of uncertainty in the premises. The ordinary way is to call squash seed dry when the enveloping skin has separated from it, and the seed itself is much contracted and also has a dry look. If the temperature to which it has been exposed is quite low, this is a pretty safe guide, but if it has been dried at a somewhat high temperature—though the seeds, when handled, may rustle with a dry sound—if such seeds are packed in barrels they will be very likely to sweat, and, when turned out, come out in caked masses, and if left together soon become musty. Squash seed, to be really dry, must be so in the meat as well as in the shell, and this can be in a moment determined by endeavoring to bend them. If they are pliable, they are not yet sufficiently dry ; if they snap instead of bending, they can be safely stored for future use.

How long will Squash Seed keep its Vitality ?—Squash seed is, like all other seed, best kept in a cool place, where the air is dry and the temperature as even as possible. I have found that those which were kept in an open bag did not retain their vitality so long by a year, as those which were kept in the same bag, but placed in paper packages.

I have known squash seed to be fairly good at six years old, and again to be worthless when but three years old, and with no perceptible difference in the getting out and method of keeping. I would lay down the rule to always test squash seed before planting, if it be over two years old. This can be easily done by placing a few in a cup, with water sufficient to swell them, covering them with some cotton wool, to prevent evaporation, and setting the cup near the stove or on the upper shelf of a closet where the heat is gentle.

If the oil that enters into the composition of the meat of the squash seed has become rancid, the vegetative power of the seed is destroyed. This is easily determined by breaking the seed, when the meat will be of dark color, and have a rancid taste. Under such circumstances, the shell of the spoiled seed will usually be darker colored than that of good seed. In a lot of seed saved at the same time a portion will be spoiled, while the remainder will readily vegetate, and some that to the eye and taste appear to be perfectly sound, will prove to be utterly worthless. The cause of the difference in either case I do not know.

The proportion of seed and entrails of squashes to their entire weight is less than is generally supposed. By tests, applied towards the close of February, a few years ago, I found that the weight of seed and entrails to the entire squash, in the Turban, was as 65 to 1000 ; and, in the Hubbard, as 55 to 1000. At that date the entrails had less weight than they would have shown earlier in the season.

INSTINCTS AND HABITS OF SQUASH VINES.

It seems hardly fitting to close this treatise without alluding to something higher than the mere pecuniary or culinary value of the squash family. In common with all vegetables, the vine has instincts which are both curious and wonderful. How singular it is that roots have power to push through the soil directly to the spot where the best food is found, descending, if necessary, below the plane of growth, or ascending above it to the very surface and developing a perfect mist of rootlets to catch up the decaying particles found under a small heap of rubbish ! Still more wonderful are some of the instincts of the vine itself. Each tendril stretches out to fasten itself to something by which it can support the vine, and rarely, if ever, will it take hold of any but the best supporter within reach. Yet more strange even than this is the instinct these tendrils develop. They not only reach out for a support, and make selection of the object, but they will vary the direction of their growth through quite a number of degrees in pursuit of the particular object they have selected. To see this wonderful phenomenon in its most striking aspect, select a vine of some one of the mammoth varieties, under circumstances in which its most vigorous growth will be developed. Let every stick, weed, or the like, be removed from the vicinity of the main runner, and then thrust firmly into the ground a slip of shingle, not over half an inch wide, on one side of the vine, a few inches beyond the outstretched tendril that is always found near the extremity, noting with care at the same time the direction in which the extremity of the vine points. Within twenty-four hours it will be found that the vine has turned from its former course, towards the side on which the shingle is placed, while the

tendril has turned towards the shingle and perhaps found
and grasped it ! In proof that this is no mere chance
event, let the slip of shingle be now removed, and placed
in the same relation to the vine as before, but on the
opposite side. Within twenty-four hours the vine will
be found to have turned from its former course and to be
inclined towards the side on which the shingle is placed,
while the tendril on that side has shown a correspond-
ing movement. Then study the tendril. It is most
admirably adapted for its office ; it is usually a compound
spiral, one-half of it winding to the right and the other
half of it to the left, thus combining the greatest strength
with the greatest possible elasticity. As another illustration of its wonderful instincts, I have seen a squash vine
run about ten feet along the surface of the ground, keeping its extremity within a few inches of the surface, until
it passed under the projecting limb of a pear tree, which
was about four feet above the surface of the earth ; here
it stretched up almost vertically towards the tree, until
it had almost reached it, when, not having sufficient
stamina to support it to a further effort, it fell over
towards the ground, forming an arch. It immediately
turned up with a second effort to reach the tree, made a
second failure and formed a second arch, and with still
another failure a third arch, by which time the extremity
had passed out from under the tree, when it kept on its
horizontal growth the same as before it had reached the
tree! Such instincts are wonderful. How did the vine
know the tree was above it, or that the slip of shingle was
at either the right or left of it ?

During the best growing weather the growth of the
vine is very rapid. I have found, by actual measurement,
that a vine of a mammoth variety grew above fourteen
inches in twenty-four hours. Sometimes, during a season
of drouth, a surprising tenacity of life is displayed. I
well remember one piece of vines growing on a shallow

spot above a ledge, where, during a season of severe drouth, I could find nothing but earth as dry as dust, close down to the ledge ; yet these vines, for more than a week, would wilt and apparently dry up each day, to renew themselves with the dews over night.   I have very rarely (and I have often examined them for this,) found the tendrils of the squash vine seizing on the Apple of Peru (Strammonium,) a large weed quite common near the sea shore, of disagreeable odor and poisonous in its nature, when taken internally.   Now, the Apple of Peru is very common in our squash fields, and presents the most stable support of all the weeds of the field.   Then why this apparent antipathy ?

EVAPORATING, CANNING, AND COOKING THE SQUASH.

Within a few years, a large business has been developed in the Eastern States in the evaporating and canning of squashes.   These processes enable housewives to bridge the interval between spring and fall, and bring this fine vegetable to their tables in the form of pie all the year.   When carefully put up, the evaporated squash makes as good a pie as when used fresh-gathered from the vine.   The extent of the canning business may be inferred from the fact that when, in its infancy, I supplied a Boston firm with thirty tons of squashes, from which the seeds had been removed, to be used for this purpose, they informed me that they had already used for canning three hundred tons that season.   A single suggestion, drawn from personal experience, to those who may find a market for their seeded squashes: When sending them by railroad, unless the weather is below freezing, be sure and have the door of the car open an inch or two, for squashes, when seeded, are very apt to develop heat.   A word about the cooking of the hard-shelled varieties. Do not attempt to remove the shell, but, after breaking to a convenient size, cook by steam, instead of boiling. In bringing it to the table, the flesh is generally scraped from the shell, but this is not the best way. To preserve the fine grain of the squash, and keep its dryness, bring it to the table on the shell, and so serve it, with the shell as a natural dish. We have oysters on the shell; and why not squash ? The old saying that " the nearer the bone, the sweeter the meat," may or may not be true, but we know from personal experience, dating from the time when we could first handle a knife with safety, that the nearer the shell, the finer, richer, and dryer is the squash.

I have endeavored to make my little treatise as complete a manual as possible. If, from the directions given, so delicious a vegetable as the squash shall be more generally and more successfully cultivated, I shall be well pleased.

INDEX.

(81)

NEW AMERICAN FARM BOOK.

ORIGINALLY BY

R. L. ALLEN,

AUTHOR OF "DISEASES OF DOMESTIC ANIMALS," AND FORMERLY EDITOR OF
THE "AMERICAN AGRICULTURIST."

REVISED AND ENLARGED BY

LEWIS F. ALLEN,

AUTHOR OF "AMERICAN CATTLE," EDITOR OF THE "AMERICAN SHORT-HOR
HERD BOOK," ETC.

CONTENTS:

SENT POST-PAID, PRICE $2.50.

ORANGE JUDD COMPANY,

751 Broadway, New-York.

Keeping One Cow.

Being the Experience of a Number of Practical Writers, in a Clear and Condensed Form, upon the

MANAGEMENT OF A SINGLE MILCH COW.

Illustrated with Full Page Engravings of the most Famous Dairy Cows.

NOTICES BY THE PRESS.

Designed to show the utility of every family (where it is at all practicable) keeping its own cow. The testimony given is that of the experience of quite a number of well-known writers and practical men, and the subject is one of particular interest to a large proportion of our people.— *Cincinnati Live Stock Review.*

Pure, rich, fresh, wholesome milk is such an important matter in a family, especially one where there are young children, that a good service has been rendered by showing how it can be produced in abundance at the cheapest rates. The volume, of convenient size, is attractively made with a number of illustrations, among which are portraits of eight famous dairy cows, one of them being a cow belonging to Queen Victoria, and now kept at the Shaw Farm, Windsor Home Par — *The Evening Mail,* New York.

The Volume is edited by Col. Mason C. Weld, and Prof. Manly Miles, authorities on dairy matters. Soils, crops, stables, care of manure, soiling, care of cow and calf, and every conceivable point connected with the subject, are treated of under a score of different circumstances, and bring to the reader a variety of methods from which to select.— *Standard,* New Bedford, Mass.

Composed of contributions from fifteen or sixteen writers on points connected with the subject, selected from nearly 100 papers submitted for the purpose....The work is illustrated with a number of portraits of famous dairy cows of different breeds, and some other engravings of buildings, etc.— *Cultivator and Country Gentleman,* Albany, N. Y.

This book represents the individual experiences and advice of acknowledged authorities, and is designed to show that every family should have its own cow. The list of contributors to it embraces Mr. Henry E. Alvord, of Massachusetts; Prof. D. D. Slade, of Harvard College; Mr. P. S. Norris, of New York; Mr. Geo. G. Duffie, of Alabama; and other writers of prominence. Mr. Orange Judd adds a chapter from his individual experience. — *Indiana Farmer,* Indianapolis, Ind.

CLOTH, PRICE, POST-PAID, $1.00.

SILOS AND ENSILAGE:

The Preservation of Fodder Corn and Other Green Fodder Crops. Bringing together the most recent information, from various sources.

Edited by DR. GEORGE THURBER.

Dr. Thurber's eminent reputation as a horticulturist and agriculturist must secure a wide sale for this volume among farmers, who are now so actively interested in the construction of silos.

Fully Illustrated. PRICE, POST-PAID, 50 CENTS.

ORANGE JUDD CO., 751 Broadway, N. Y.

Gardening for Young and Old.

THE

CULTIVATION OF GARDEN VEGETABLES IN THE FARM GARDEN.

By JOSEPH HARRIS, M.S.,

Author of "Walks and Talks on the Farm," "Harris on the Pig," "Talks on Manures," etc.

CONTENTS.

Introduction.—An Old and a New Garden.—Gardening for Boys.--How to Begin.—Preparing the Soil.—Killing the Weeds.—About High Farming.—Competition in Crops.—The Manure Question.—The Implements Needed.—Starting Plants in the House or in the Hot-bed.—The Window-box.—Making the Hot-bed.—Cold Frames.—Insects.—The Use of Poisons.—The Care of Poisons.—The Cultivation of Vegetables in the Farm Garden.—The Cultivation of Flowers.

ILLLUSTRATED.

12mo. Cloth. Price, post-paid, $1.25.

ORANGE JUDD COMPANY, 751 Broadway, New York,

LIBRARY OF CONGRESS

0 000 916 489 3

The American Agriculturist

FOR THE

Farm, Garden, and Household.

Established in 1842.

The Best and Cheapest Agricultural Journal in the World.

TERMS, which include postage *pre-paid* by the Publishers: $1.50 per annum, in advance ; 3 copies for $4 ; 4 copies for $5 ; 5 copies for $6 ; 6 copies for $7 ; 7 copies for $8 ; 10 or more copies, only $1 each. Single Numbers, 15 cents.

AMERIKANISCHER AGRICULTURIST.

The only purely Agricultural German paper in the United States, and the best in the world. It contains all of the principal matter of the English Edition, together with special departments for German cultivators, prepared by writers trained for the work. Terms same as for the " American Agriculturist."

BOOKS FOR FARMERS AND OTHERS.

Send ten cents for our new handsomely illustrated and descriptive Catalogue of Books on all branches of Agriculture, Horticulture, Architecture, etc. All books comprised in this Catalogue will be mailed pre-paid on receipt of the price named. Our abridged descriptive Catalogue of Books will be sent free on application.

Books on Out-Door Sports and Pastimes.

Send five cents for our new and elegantly gotten up SPORTSMAN'S COM-PANION, containing brief descriptions or outlines of nearly one hundred and eighty works upon legitimate Out-door Sports and Amusements, and illustrat-ed with a great number of engravings, many of them drawn from life, and faithfully portraying the points and characteristics of game, birds, fishes, horses, dogs, etc., etc.

ORANGE JUDD COMPANY, 751 Broadway, New York.

Made in the USA
Las Vegas, NV
14 April 2024

88690039R00052